MUSIC ADVOCACY AND STUDENT LEADERSHIP
Key Components of Every Successful Music Program

A Collection of Writings

ALSO BY

Tim Lautzenheiser

The Joy of Inspired Teaching

The Art of Successful Teaching

MUSIC ADVOCACY AND STUDENT LEADERSHIP

KEY COMPONENTS OF EVERY SUCCESSFUL MUSIC PROGRAM

A Collection of Writings

Tim Lautzenheiser

GIA Publications, Inc.
Chicago

Portions of this book have been reprinted from
Music Express, published by Hal Leonard, and
Teaching Music through Performance in Band,
volumes 1 through 4, published by GIA Publications,
Inc. Reprinted with perimission.

Music Advocacy and Student Leadership
Key Components of Every Successful Music Program
A Collection of Writings
Tim Lautzenheiser

G-6531
Copyright © 2005, GIA Publications, Inc.
7404 S. Mason Ave., Chicago, IL 60638
www.giamusic.com
ISBN: 1-57999-477-6

Cover design/illustration Yolanda Durán
Book design Yolanda Durán

Printed in the United States of America.

Dedication

This book, along with everything else I've ever written, is dedicated to all those students, colleagues, and music boosters/parents who have supported our workshops, seminars, clinics, and various events for over two decades. Nobody trains to be a professional clinician. You cannot major in music advocacy. My career has been an expedition that has opened doors of opportunity I never knew existed, and it has provided the chance to work with the very finest people on the planet. The debt board will forever rest heavily in your favor; THANK YOU!

CONTENTS

PART ONE
Advocacy for Music Educators

PART TWO
Advocacy for Music Education

PART THREE

The Selection and Development of Effective Student Leaders

PART FOUR

The Band Director as a Leader

Author's Thoughts

First and foremost, THANK YOU for choosing to spend your valuable time perusing *Music Advocacy and Student Leadership: Key Components of Every Successful Music Program*. The following pages represent a compilation of writings addressing important "off the podium" responsibilities.

We know the vast majority of music makers learn the language of music in the school setting. We also know every child has the propensity to learn music. Therefore, the role of the music educator becomes a crucial factor in the development of every person who enters the school culture. Not only does music make the difference, but the music teacher is the person who is instrumental in making that difference.

Hopefully this book will provide some useable ideas you can adapt to your own situation. From raising community awareness about the importance of arts education to creating a workable blueprint for positive student leadership, I am certain there is something you will find that can support your professional goals and your personal mission.

This isn't a book you should read from cover-to-cover. Instead, look through the chapter index and find the subject area that fits your needs at the given time. Perhaps you are preparing your student leaders for a new semester and you want to increase their understanding of what their role should be; you will find a healthy library of ideas to accommodate this endeavor. Or you may need to enlighten a group of soon-to-be music parents concerning the immeasurable value music learning will have in preparing their child for all aspects of life's challenges; again, there is compelling and convincing data to support your recruitment efforts. There are even some special topics designed "just for you."

Thank you again for your commitment and dedication to this very special profession. It is a privilege to join you along the pathway to excellence, and it is an honor to have you add this reference book to your personal library.

Let the music begin!

Acknowledgements

Books don't just "happen." There are many people who have contributed to this project; it is truly a labor of love, or rather a process of love. Allow me to extend special "bravos" to those who truly "deserve the credit."

To Alec Harris, president of GIA Publications, Inc., who has been an incredible friend from the first day we met. His support and encouragement are second to none. There would never have been a first book without Alec's involvement, and now we are at book three and counting. Thank you, Alec; you set the bar high for all of us.

To Marguerite ("Rite") Wilder, editor and organizer extraordinaire, who took on the daunting task of putting the various chapters together. Rite is one of my all-time favorite people because of her positive energy combined with her desire to spread the joy of music-making to young and old alike. It would be great if every child could have the experience of working with Ms. Wilder; if so, every child would be involved in music. Thank you, Rite; you did it again!

To Herman Knoll, senior vice president of Hal Leonard, Inc., for graciously giving his permission so we could adapt several of the chapters from articles written for Hal Leonard's publication Music Express. Herman's own successful career as a music educator/band director serves as the basis for his willingness to do whatever it takes to avail people to the value of music education. Thank you, Herman; you are a highly respected colleague, but—even more—you are a cherished friend.

To Paula Crider and Dr. Joe Scagnoli for adding their words of support in the **Foreword** and the **Introduction.** They represent the best in the business—and then some. So much of this book is a reflection of their contributions to our music world. Paula and "Scagger," here's to many more mutual projects in the future.

To Andrea Price, my mate, my partner, my confidant, and clearly the reason I have been able to spend much of my professional life working with music students, music teachers, and music parents. None of these projects would have ever come to fruition without Andrea's remarkable wisdom and unconditional love. Thank you, thank you, thank you.

Foreword
by Paula Crider

On extremely rare occasions, we may be privileged to encounter a unique and special individual who can dramatically change our perceptions, a person who will elevate thinking to new levels, rekindle fires long forgotten, and cause us to see the world as it should be. In this lifetime, for millions of students, teachers, and lovers of music, that person is Tim Lautzenheiser. Tim's incomparable gifts defy verbal description, but when he speaks, we are immediately aware of the fact that we are in the presence of genius.

Tim's first two publications, *The Art of Successful Teaching: A Blend of Context and Content* and *The Joy of Inspired Teaching,* have had a profound effect upon our profession. These eloquent and informative books provide both wisdom by which we may become better teachers and rare but much-needed inspiration for the musical soul. *Music Advocacy and Student Leadership* is destined to become an invaluable resource for music educators as well.

It is perhaps understandable that we music educators tend to bury our heads in the seemingly insurmountable sands of never ending teaching demands, reasoning that there is no time to research facts needed to defend the musical arts. However, gentle reader, if we do not become active advocates for our profession . . . who will? Within the pages of this book, Tim provides sources and resources, a "blueprint for advocacy success." His perspective, once embraced, proves so compelling that we never see things in quite the same way again. Nor should we have any excuse not to become leaders in the quest to take our profession to the next level of musical excellence.

With intuition, insight, inspiration, and conviction, Tim Lautzenheiser views the musical arts through the mirror of positive reflection. Tim has an unrivaled ability to reach the heart of matters in an honest, concise, and engaging manner. He helps us to see that which is essential and moves us to cultivate a lasting passion for the teaching of music. Tim embodies the very essence of commitment to excellence. He challenges us to take the road less traveled, and in doing so, we discover the boundless joys the journey may bring.

I am honored to contribute this foreword and privileged to call Tim my friend.

Because of this book, you are armed with invaluable knowledge . . . may it move you to action!

About Paula Crider

My heartfelt thanks are extended to Paula Crider for sharing her important thoughts and feelings as part of this book's **Foreword**. Paula is an exemplary role model for every educator of every subject. She is not only an innately gifted musician, an artistic maestro, and a remarkable leader, but a master teacher who boldly reminds us that we must "walk our talk with integrity and class." Nobody does that better than my adopted sister, Paula Crider.

From her years as a public school band director through her tenure at the University of Texas, her career is vividly marked with one success after another. However, she will quickly redirect the credit and compliments to her students and her colleagues, yet another of her signature character attributes.

Great mentors not only fill our minds with valuable information, but they fill our hearts with inspiration and desire. This special *magic* is truly a gift of untold value. Paula "has the gift," and she has dedicated her life to unselfishly *giving* to countless people who have been fortunate enough to know her and to work with her.

Introduction
by Joseph Scagnoli

Never before has the need for advocacy and strong leadership in music and the arts been more important to us than during this time of changing educational trends.

This special book helps all music educators bring the value of what they accomplish and what music and the arts can do for all students to the attention of the general public by making the facts known about the wonderful experiences of a musical life.

Earl Dunn, professor of music emeritus and director of bands emeritus at Ball State University (and a mentor to both Tim and me) often commented that there is no course offered for our future music educators that includes the ideas and techniques for effective marketing and good public relations strategies. However, there *are* many music educators who seem to know how to employ successful advocacy strategies for their programs, and we can all benefit from the guidelines offered in the chapters ahead.

In fact, in the not-so-distant past, the idea of promoting music programs and the valuable experiences provided to students by music teachers was looked at as contrary to being a true professional. The purist professional (of previous decades) thought the "true professional" was one whose work would immediately be recognized by the public without any public relations effort.

All of this being said, think of today's media-driven marketing world, which has evolved over the past decades. Shouldn't we employ effective promotional techniques and advocacy strategies to keep the importance of music and the arts in public spotlight? Shouldn't everyone understand the value of music education? The answer to these questions has to be a resounding "yes!"

The idea of eliminating music and the arts during the school day and placing them either before or after school (to make more time available for "academic" subjects) certainly emphasizes the point that teachers of music and the arts need to take a more proactive approach. The general public must be made aware of the value of what we teach and how it positively impacts the overall education of our students.

As a society, we are more comfortable in how we objectively weigh and measure things than we are with the subjective process of how we express our feelings. It is in this subjective area that we must be stronger advocates for music and the arts, an area that by its nature allows for differences to exist. For the pure scientist, these differences are viewed as uncomfortable "loose ends," and must be resolved to reflect one interpretation or singular outcome. However, music and the arts by their very nature are subjective and create and encourage the opportunity for various interpretations.

Herein lies the true value of what Tim brings to all of us; he has personally lived and experienced all he advocates and suggests in this book. He has taken the time to put his thoughts in order to explain the importance of not only what we do, but its value to our students and to our society. Tim's credibility stems from his extensive travel and contact with thousands of music educators throughout the country. The ideas presented in each of the chapters of this timely offering have come to fruition through the reality of Tim's own life experiences and the students, teachers, and people who have influenced his thinking. In fact, all the leadership and advocacy ideas in the book literally jump off the page in the same energetic style we have come to expect from Tim and his always-proactive approach.

As Tim explains, to choose *excellence* as your pathway in life is not to have chosen the easiest pathway, but to have chosen one that is fraught with risk and the uneasiness of possible failure; however, it is the pathway to success.

When I think of my dear friend Tim Lautzenheiser and the lifetime of various experiences we have shared, I am always aware of the conscious decision he made to help others find excellence in their own lives. In all the times I had the pleasure of hearing Tim teach the Leadership in the Arts course (during his tenure at Ball State University), his approach to developing excellence was never ending. In all the quotes used by Tim to make certain important points, the old adage "Actions speak louder than words" is the most fitting to reflect his strong leadership and commitment to excellence; this is the ultimate compliment to a master teacher.

As everyone knows, Tim is not only a wonderful friend, but he is someone who strives to be a role model to all who want to improve their teaching and life skills. With Tim, the glass is always half full and ripe with potential and opportunities to improve the so-called "status quo." His valuable mission will always be a work-in-progress.

About Dr. Joe Scagnoli

Dr. Joe Scagnoli, director of bands and associate director of the School of Music at Ball State University, is one of those uniquely talented conductors who can bring an ensemble to extraordinary musical heights, and then immediately step off the podium and embrace the responsibilities of a visionary administrator.

There is a reason "Doc's" students continue to serve as leaders in the music world: they have learned from a teacher who wraps every bit of knowledge with a sincerity that is certain to last a lifetime. Joe Scagnoli is the ultimate teacher's teacher, while being an avid student who is constantly learning, growing, and becoming. He brings a powerful recipe of success to those who are his students and colleagues.

Dr. Scagnoli and I are both Ball State University graduates, had the same mentor (Mr. Earl Dunn), now teach at our alma mater, and think learning music is the best gift any child could ever receive.

Of the many special qualities Dr. Scagnoli brings to every situation, none is more honorable or more noteworthy than his sense of *loyalty*. It is the best of all human traits, and it is often forgotten in our haste to reach our given goals. Thank you, Joe ("Scagger"), for always reminding us how important we are to one another; you live what this book is about, and you do it with *class*.

PART ONE
Advocacy for Music Educators

Chapter 1

Dealing with "It's Good Enough...!"

*When we think positively and imagine what
we want, we risk disappointment; when
we don't, we ensure it.*

Lana Limpert

▪ Doesn't the title make you cringe?

▪ Isn't the phrase, "It's good enough," offensive to your
sense of educational integrity?

▪ Aren't you tempted to impulsively react in a defensive
manner when a student resorts to this worn-out old excuse?

Why would any musician (or anyone, for that matter) ever
claim "it's good enough?" We know the pathway to excellence is never-ending, and yet we are constantly searching
for teaching techniques that will stimulate our students to
reach a higher level of personal achievement, to push them
beyond the perceived "it's good enough."

Without question, every individual has an unlimited supply of
undeveloped (or underdeveloped) talent. Even the master
performers are constantly pushing themselves to a higher
level of skill attainment. If we know we can be more proficient,

what keeps us from developing to the next level of musical awareness, performance, or understanding? Isn't this the same inquiry we have concerning our students? Why don't they practice, invest, commit, dedicate, and enjoy the benefits of their efforts?

Humans, by nature, enjoy comfort. In addition to that, we are creatures of habit, and we find ourselves repeating behaviors simply for the sake of fulfilling the requirements of life; in a sense, we do what we do to maintain the status quo or to get to the point of "it's good enough." Therefore, our students replicate the behavior by learning what they need to learn to meet the assigned goals, play/sing the chosen music, and complete the requested objectives; it is rare to find those who overachieve or push themselves beyond the targeted finish line.

Instead of focusing on what motivates the individual (in other words, what it takes to stir one to push beyond the given requirements), perhaps we should look at what is holding the person back? What is it that hinders the forward momentum of our students or us? The world of psychology spotlights two specific areas that impede us in our quest for quality: fear of failure and fear of success.

Fear of failure. It is easy to understand the hesitation to leave oneself vulnerable to failure. We have learned to avoid failure at all costs along with the embarrassing emotional pain that accompanies this dreaded outcome. Instead of seeing failure as a stepping stone to achievement, we often see it as a termination point. However, the most successful people we know have all embraced the concept of failure and, in fact, have even used it as a motivating force to accept, correct, and retry the task at hand. There will never be success without failure; therefore, failure must be reframed in our understanding as part of the formula to help us reach our highest goals and aspirations.

Fear of success. Why would someone be frightened at the prospect of success? Isn't that what we are trying to achieve? Isn't that the pay-off for all of our hard work? Ah yes, but success brings along some companions that are not always part of our comfort zone.

- **More responsibility:** A successful person will be expected to uphold the level of responsibility needed to maintain the achieved standard.

- **Higher expectations:** Winners are expected to keep winning. In most cases this means going beyond the level of the initial success.

- **Being in the limelight:** Successful people are seen and heard by all. There is no place to hide; others are always scrutinizing those who are successful.

- **The long fall to the next failure:** When the successful person faces the inevitable failure, the distance to the bottom of the mountain is greater than it is for those who do not try at all.

- **Separation from friends:** Success often creates a chasm between the individual and the rest of the crowd. Peer pressure often serves as the deciding factor in whether to push the extra mile or not; it is easier to stay with the crowd and play it safe.

Based on the two expressed fears (failure/success), the most comfortable place to be is "it's good enough." The mind logically concludes, "Do what you have to do to avoid failure, but be careful not to catapult yourself to a high level of success."

To counteract this reasoning, we, as educators, must be the first to model the benefits of both failure and success. In other words, we must be willing to set the pace by demonstrating our own willingness to push the envelope of possibility. Failure (that results from an effort to achieve) needs to be rewarded with guided encouragement to "learn from the mistakes" and then use the newly discovered data as we make a second, third, and fourth attempt. Success (resulting from a calculated effort) needs to be acknowledged immediately, followed by the assurance that the value of the learning process was more important than the achieved product or outcome.

Students will reach beyond "it's good enough" when they understand there are personal benefits to both failure and success; we, as educators, must reinforce this behavior to insure the positive seeking of higher levels of proficiency becomes an integral part of our students' behavior.

The only time "it's good enough" is when we decide to take action on the fact that it's *not* good enough.

Chapter 2

Keeping Good Time

The purpose of man is action, not thought.

Thomas Carlyle

We all know the pathway to excellence requires a high level of commitment and dedication. There is no shortcut to quality. In the musical world, we are faced with the challenge of leading our students to the highest peaks of artistic proficiency while dealing with the reality that these are the young men and women who have chosen to embrace the world of music in addition to all their other academic responsibilities. The dilemma is obvious: How do we reach any kind of mastery without slighting some other aspect of the growth and development of the student?

Today's world moves at a fast pace. Society is "instant gratification" oriented. We can order a product online prior to going to sleep, and it will be waiting for us at the front door when we wake up in the morning. The buy-now-pay-later mentality has become a way of life. Unfortunately, the process of "making music" (or perhaps any substantive educational endeavor) requires the investment of *time*. One cannot hurry-up and learn to play sixteenth notes or take a crash course in the key of F-sharp. Making great music is labor-intensive, and the one element we need for success is TIME.

As school curricula evolve, there are more and more additional learning options available to the students. It's no longer just sports, music, and theater. Every discipline has developed an outside-the-school-day agenda, from the debate club to the National Honor Society; there is a huge demand on every student's time. We are well aware of the academic status of the music students; they represent the best-of-the-best. They are also the people who are involved in the debate club and the officers of the National Honor Society. This is all well and good, but the equalizer is the reality that we are limited to twenty-four hours in each day. No level of intelligence or clever time management can alter this fundamental certainty.

Because of the finite amount of time available to our students, choices must be made. Unfortunately, when we (as music teachers) are inflexible about our demands on their time, some students will simply choose to *not* participate. The days of, "It's either my way or the highway," could well find many students hitting the open road. This is not to say we should turn our backs on the importance of being responsible to the agreed contract of the requisite of time. We do, however, need to become more organized in our efforts to be more *efficient* and *effective* in the use of our time and the time of our students.

The puzzle of *time management* is one that continues to receive ongoing attention in every aspect of life. Corporations spend huge amounts of revenue to uncover and discover the best use of their employee's time. The ultimate question is: How can we make the very best use of the allotted amount of time? This is also a valid inquiry for music educators; we are always wanting more time. We are always thinking, if we just had another week of rehearsals, etc. Knowing this is wishful thinking, perhaps we should focus on making the most of the given time.

Creating a plan. There is no substitute for a great plan. It is easy to fall victim to the all-too-familiar "we can make it up as we go" syndrome. Certainly, the master teachers are able to shift directions along the way, but knowing the timeline, having the benchmarks, and working within the framework of a well-thought-out plan creates a sense of security for all concerned.

Developing a long-range calendar. Some schools require everyone to engage in this process of calendar planning. If students (and parents) have the wherewithal to *know* what is expected in terms of attendance, performance schedules, and rehearsal expectations, it removes much of the stress caused by last-minute scheduling. We must be sensitive to other facets of the growth process: family reunions, church events, weddings, religious holidays, and so forth. Certainly there will be exceptions along the way; however, there is a feeling of cooperative understanding when parents are aware of what lies ahead.

Communicate with parents. There are no flawless templates that can or will sidestep unexpected occurrences. When a student is unable to attend a required event, it could be for a number of reasons, some of which are better than others. It is often tempting to confront the student instead of starting a conversation with the parent(s). If the members of the group understand that we, as teachers, are there to support them by creating an understanding with their parents, it removes the guilt and stress often shouldered by the student. It is not unusual for a young musician to simply quit the ensemble rather than face an inflexible teacher.

Seek a win-win solution. We must ask ourselves, "What is best for the student?" Yes, there are implications that will affect other members of the organization (particularly in the field of music), but what will benefit the student in the overall scheme of life? "Can the make-up test be rescheduled? If so, then let me go to your chemistry teacher and help you solve the problem." (In other words, become the conduit for the resolution.) There are students who will go to any length to avoid reporting the conflict; they do not want to disappoint anyone, and as a result of this kind of logic they end up disappointing everyone, including themselves. Let your students (and parents) know there is always a win-win solution if everyone works together for the welfare of those involved.

Be a mature role model. While we have all witnessed the melodramatic reactions of the irate educator who is incensed by the lack of loyalty, or the inability of the students to see the negative ramifications to the organization, these emotional outbursts rarely bring anything to a calm understanding. In fact, the problem is often escalated, and this poor reaction jeopardizes any chance of creating a viable solution. This is not to suggest that we should not express disappointment, but the energies should be directed toward finding a workable plan for the present *and* used as a learning opportunity for the future.

Extending your appreciation. Regardless of the outcome of the situation, we are wise to send a note of thanks to all those who were a part of the scenario. Not only does it demonstrate our willingness to be open in the communication, it helps create a positive forum of exchange for the future. Silence can be deafening, and if we simply acknowledge everyone and express our appreciation for the use of "their time" we are developing a strong network of cooperation for times ahead. Yes, there will be more conflicts.

As the years pass, time becomes more valuable. As music educators, our greed for *more time* may need to be replaced by our greed for a *better use of the time we have.* This means we have to be alert concerning the use of our students' time, and be willing to adjust to accommodate the unknowns that are certain to come our way.

We have all had mentors who told us we needed to "keep good time" if we ever wanted to be successful in the field of music. Perhaps there was more to their advice than merely matching the tic-tock of a metronome.

Chapter 3

Wanted: Music Teachers for the Present and Future

The best time to plant a tree is twenty years ago; the next best time is now!

African proverb

Over the decades, music education has faced some very difficult and systemic challenges, from outcome-based education to block scheduling; however, creative ingenuity, coupled with a missionary work ethic, has been the key to keeping music as a mainstay in our school curriculums. Masterminds continue to take the present curriculum/scheduling mandates and discover a workable combination to ensure the welfare of our school music programs. Although this is an ongoing and often uphill climb, we know there is a groundswell of support for "music in our schools" thanks to the undying efforts and energies of teachers, parents, and music advocates who understand the vital importance of the arts as a cornerstone of every holistic educational blueprint.

The emphasis on music advocacy is a reflection of the work of MENC (The National Association for Music Education), NAMM (The International Music Products Association), and NARAS (The National Association of Recording Arts and Sciences). Coalition programs were established throughout the country to create a grassroots communication network to specifically inform and educate people about the extended benefits of music education. Many of these programs are still very active; we enjoy countless stories of music programs being saved because of the convincing library of information available via the state and national coalition organizations. The increased participation in school music reflects a new public awareness of the value of music learning, and much of the credit goes to the coalition efforts.

While there are isolated cases of endangered music programs, there is a public consciousness that did not exist ten years ago. All-in-all, we are gaining ground in our quest; that's the good news. However, we have to guard against complacency; clearly, music advocacy should not be a reactionary device to a threatened music curriculum, but a pro-active tool that becomes a pillar of every music education offering.

In our quest to save music in our schools, the focus has been on the welfare of the students and the security of the music curriculum. All the while, we assumed everything was solidly in place with the music educators; we now are facing a dual problem of: (1) a music teacher shortage and (2) an alarming attrition rate of those who are part of the music education profession. What irony: we heightened the public interest and created more candidates to be music-makers, but we now have a void in our supply of qualified music educators.

This is the classic problematic situation posed to every business/marketing student regarding supply and demand. What are the long term and short term solutions to this predicament? Let us assume that for the sake of an agreed upon outcome we will not consider reducing the demand as an option; in other words, we will not turn our backs on the students who wish to be a part of a thriving and successful music program. (In essence, this would be a reversal of all the music advocacy efforts to date.) By the process of deductive logic, we must then focus on a twofold answer:

1. **Short-term:** retain the qualified educators who are presently in the music classrooms.

2. **Long-term:** recruit outstanding candidates to consider music education as a lifelong profession.

In response to part one, we must first ask, "Why **are** young teachers leaving the educational world to pursue other interests?" (It is not only in the field of music, but throughout all of education.) Rather than speculate on this answer, I polled several former music educators who spent less than three years in the classroom/rehearsal room. Their answers to the following three questions were much the same:

A. What was the primary reason that you chose to be a music educator?

B. Why did you decide to leave the profession after your short tenure?

C. Do you have any suggestions as to how we might better prepare the new teachers?

The following explanations are a compilation of their responses and paraphrased for a more concise understanding.

To the person, the answers were aligned; in fact, they were remarkably similar.

    A. What was the primary reason you chose to be a music educator?

In every case, the most influential factor was a former teacher.

> *I chose to be a music teacher (choir/band/orchestra director) because of my teacher. I had a mentor who encouraged my participation in music and guided me through the college selection process.*

It is apparent that many college music education students are planning to replicate the life of their high school role models, in this case, their music teachers. Therefore, we know the long-term solution is to be found in today's teachers. Is it the love of music or the admiration for the teacher that is the foundation of this important life choice? Perhaps both; regardless, it is obvious that the music teachers of today are the source for the music teachers of tomorrow. This responsibility must become a priority in our work; we want to keep a keen eye for those students who demonstrate the qualities and attributes of an exemplary music educator.

    B. Why did you decide to leave the profession after your short tenure?

The replies to the second question should give us some insight concerning the "what they expect" when entering the teaching world and "what they get."

I had no idea I would spend so much time taking care of things outside of the music teaching. I didn't understand how to deal with budgets, schedules, other faculty members, administrators, and the ongoing responsibilities that just showed up every day. I found myself living in constant stress because I couldn't get everything accomplished. It was great working with the students making music, but that was such a small part of my day. There were so many things out of my control, and I didn't have anyone to turn to for help.

Most likely these sentiments are true for every first-, second-, or third-year teacher; however, why do some people work through these conditions while others simply walk away? May I suggest the answer could well lie in the last thought of the above quote: *"I didn't have anyone to turn to for help."* We have much evidence to support the notion that teacher-mentors have great success in serving as counselor/guides for the beginning educator. Veteran teachers "know the ropes." An open ear coupled with some gentle advice could be the perfect combination for "saving a teacher." Doctors have an extended internship, and pilots fly many years before assuming the captain's seat; there is much to be said for these professional training templates.

C. Do you have any suggestions as to how we might better prepare the new teachers?

While everyone agrees there is no substitute for "on-the-job training," short of recreating the curriculum for music education as an apprenticeship, there are some areas we can highlight as skill-development alongside the music requisites.

> *My preparation for teaching music was excellent, but I did not have any idea how much time would be spent talking to parents, individual students, other faculty members, and just people in general. So much of my day was spent communicating about non-music things, and I didn't know how to organize my time to get everything accomplished. The frustration was not with the music, but with the other aspects of my teaching load.*

The business community recognizes the importance of "people skills," the ability to communicate in an efficient and effective manner. In reading the concerns of our "lost colleagues," we can benefit from their suggestions by focusing on interpersonal skills. We all have an endless capacity to expand our communication talents/skills.

Part of teacher training should emphasize the crucial need for listening skills, assertion skills, conflict-resolution skills, and collaborative problem-solving skills. These are fundamental in establishing and maintaining positive relationships. Poor communication skills inevitably lead to professional ineffectiveness. If we do not prepare our teachers accordingly, the "communication overwhelm" only adds to their feelings of personal disappointment and lack of accomplishment. We must focus on developing people skills as part of fundamental teacher preparation.

From an overall perspective, there is an opportunity for all of us to serve as contributors to the teacher shortage dilemma. Here are some suggestions we can put into effect immediately:

- **Recruitment.** We begin to plant seeds for the future by informing our students of the personal and professional benefits of being a music educator.

- **Retention.** We can befriend the new music teachers and serve as a reference-mentor during the early years of their careers.

- **Communication.** We must continue our own efforts to model better communication habits. The resolution to nearly every problem lies in some form of communication.

- **Advocacy.** We must take every opportunity to inform every facet of our society about the importance of music learning for EVERY child.

While these suggestions may appear to be simplistic or general in nature, I suggest that they will serve the purposeful future of our professional welfare by allowing each of us to customize our application of these goals according to the specific wants and needs of our individual schools and communities. After all, we are teachers. Teachers teaching teachers: what a powerful formula for the positive welfare of music education, and one we can put into effect immediately.

Chapter 4

Where Are the Music Educators of Tomorrow?

Ability *is what you're capable of doing.*

Motivation *determines what you do.*

Attitude *determines how well you do it.*

We have more music teaching positions available than we have music educators. With the increased focus on the benefits of music learning combined with the anticipated increase in school population, we are facing a professional crisis. We need qualified music educators, and we need them now.

Perhaps the following will offer some suggestions to insure the welfare of music education for our children, our grand-children, and many generations to follow.

How do you respond when one of your students says to you, "I want to be a music teacher. I think it would exciting to spend my life working with young musicians. Do you think it is a good idea for me to pursue music education as a career?" What is your reaction to this all-important inquiry?

First and foremost, we must be thrilled with the fact we, as music teachers, have such a lasting impact on our students, perhaps more than any other educator in their lives. The student's message in the above paragraph is quite clear: "I want to be just like *you* when I grow up." Isn't it the greatest compliment you could possibly receive? Second, it provides a forum of extended-confidence, demonstrating an individual's complete trust in you as more than a classroom teacher, but also as a mentor, a confidant, and a valued guide along life's journey. Your response can and will make a significant difference in the direction of the individual's future.

Herein lies an opportunity to graciously thank the student for considering the field of music as a career option. Again, your influence has been a key to creating this professional preference. It also offers the opportunity to explain the various aspects of the occupation rarely seen by the participant; it is time to be boldly honest as you describe what lies ahead. Ask the student, "Are you willing to":

1. Prepare yourself *now* to meet the requirements for your upcoming college music program?

2. Fulfill the rigorous curriculum requisites for an undergraduate degree?

3. Embrace the added pressure of an expanded music-major schedule?

4. Deal with the demands of extended rehearsals, demanding performances, extra duties, etc.?

5. Thrive and grow in a competitive environment?

6. Set and attain high levels of personal commitment and dedication?

7. Master the people skills necessary for teaching success?

8. Understand the trade-off of revenue intake for life-mission satisfaction?

9. Find the balance of a personal and professional life?

10. Stay fresh and enthusiastic, avoiding professional burnout?

If the student is still eager to explore the "study of music," then it is time to have the heart-to-heart conversation about the often-forgotten essential elements of a successful music educator, such as:

1. A positive attitude.

2. The willingness to meet and accept extreme challenges.

3. An endless supply of energy stretching from early morning until late at night.

4. A need to control one's temper in emotionally charged situations.

5. An ongoing effort to be genuinely fair to everyone connected with the program.

6. An affable personality designed to work with all types of people.

7. Highly developed communication skills.

8. The ability to make tough decisions under challenging circumstances.

9. A basic love of music.

10. An insatiable desire and a genuine passion to teach children the art of music making.

After all this exchange, if the student looks straight into your eyes and says, "Yes, I want to be a music teacher," then put your arm around him or her and promise to help in every way possible to select the right school to make this dream come true. It will be one of the most gratifying moments of your teaching career.

Might I suggest that many of us are music teachers because of our music teachers. We have dedicated our lives to helping others experience and understand the universal language of music, much as our mentors did for us. May we do the same for our students in the spirit of giving, sharing, knowing, and becoming. As they say, "It is a gift that lasts a lifetime."

Chapter 5

You Gotta Have H.E.A.R.T.

We make a living by what we get. We make a life by what we give.

Winston Churchill

The seed of this article came from a student who was asked to write a paper about her most influential teacher. She had to describe what separated this particular educator from all those who had been a part of her school experiences. The last line of the paper succinctly and beautifully put everything into perspective with this sentence: "Above all, Mrs. Taylor had a good heart; that's what made her so special."

It has been said that we will all have two or three great teachers in our lives. For many of us, our selected mentors were our music teachers. In fact, it is probably safe to say these very special educators are responsible for everything from our career choice to our professional philosophy of music education. The roles are now reversed and we have a wonderful opportunity to positively impact our own students as they musically travel along their educational journey.

As you think about your most influential teachers, do you remember **what** they taught or the **way** they taught it? May

I suggest, for most of us, the answer will focus on the **way:** the teachers' personality, their communication style, the atmosphere they created surrounding the curriculum, etc. This is not to suggest mere "personality" can substitute for substantive curriculum content, but it does highlight the importance of the contextual aspect of every master teacher's success-formula. **Who** we are is equally as important as **what** we teach.

Let us examine the qualities and character attributes of a master teacher who has H.E.A.R.T.:

H-HONESTY

Think about the exemplary teachers you admired and respected, those you held in highest esteem. You could always trust them to be **honest** in their assessment of every situation. They respected **truth** for the sake of **truth,** and while their decisions were not always popular, they were the right choices to reinforce the basic values of ethics, integrity, and dignity. They demanded excellence at every level, and they realized building high-quality programs with high-quality people requires a foundation of honesty.

E-ENTHUSIASM

Enthusiasm is not to be confused with the shallow excitement we often associate with lack of substance; quite the contrary, the great teachers exude a passion for their work, their programs, their schools, their communities, and—most of all—their students. **Enthusiasm,** taken from the Greek language, "en theos" (in the presence of a Divine spirit), is a reflection of the teacher's desire to exchange valuable knowledge that will make a lasting impression on his or her students. Enthusiasm is the spark that ignites the learning process and stimulates intrinsic motivation, opening the mind to an unlimited number of creative processes.

A-ATTITUDE

Did you ever know a great teacher who did not have a vivid **attitude?** Like it or not, students tend to reflect the **attitude** of their teachers. Most certainly, the extraordinary teachers raise the bar of expectation while modeling a positive **attitude** of acceptance and a willingness to help others who need extra attention in the learning process. The truly great educators do not have the time or the inclination to play in the game of sarcasm and cynicism; they refrain from being involved in negative conversations and they devote their time and energies to problem resolution instead of problem recognition. They understand the power associated with a positive role model; thus, their **attitude** is primary in everything they do and everything they are.

R-RESPONSIBILITY

Master teachers understand the crucial importance of **responsibility**—"the ability to respond." They do:

What needs to be done,
when it needs to be done,

whether they want to do it or not,
without anybody asking.

The art of teaching requires a constant focus on self-discipline. Unlike many professionals, the teacher's work day never ends. Although the final school bell completes the official school day, the dedicated educator is always thinking, planning, organizing, and creating more effective and efficient ways to support program growth to benefit the students involved. They are always encouraging others to new heights of achievement, focusing the human potential to provide a healthy atmosphere for safe and meaningful learning experiences, and they are constantly recognizing and rewarding those who are making strides toward the given goals. Simply put, they are there for everyone; they are **responsible.**

T-Trustworthiness

Great educators are "worthy-of-**trust.**" They refuse to take advantage of another individual for personal gains. They do not take shortcuts or unfairly make decisions that would put another person in an uncompromising position. While they stick firmly with their convictions, they are not restricted by outdated policies or myopic rules and regulations. Master teachers are true to their word; they do what they say they will do regardless of the price they must pay. They "walk their talk." The framework of every successful program is based on the trust of the participants who are mirroring the **trustworthiness** of the teacher.

There you have it, the **H.E.A.R.T.** of great teachers: **Honesty, Enthusiasm, Attitude, Responsibility, and Trustworthiness.**

We all have the wherewithal to enjoy and live the **H.E.A.R.T.** of a great teacher. It requires a personal commitment to practicing these cornerstone characteristics as we go through our daily agendas. Would you like to be remembered as one of the "special teachers" in the lives of your students? If so, "You gotta have **H.E.A.R.T.** "

Part Two

Advocacy for Music Education

Chapter 6

Cornerstones of a Sound Education

*Every child is an artist. The problem is how to
remain an artist once we grow up.*

Pablo Picasso

- Why music?

- Why should a student choose to take on the extra responsibilities required to be engaged in music learning?

- Why should parents encourage their children to participate
  in the school music program?

- Is there more to this than "meets the eye?"

As music educators we can all speak to the artistic reasons
to be involved in the lifelong study of music making. There is
no substitute for the language of music, and we, as members
of this profession, subscribe to the idea of "music for the
sake of music." This is all well and good if we are communicating with people who are somewhat familiar with the
music culture. It is far more difficult to be as convincing
about our mission if our listeners/audiences are not attuned
to the many benefits of music making or have no prior musical
experiences in their own lives.

Ongoing research continues to evidence *why* music students are academically stronger, and why they are the high achievers in all aspects of the educational community. The relationship is not accidental, coincidental, or even incidental. There is a definite, measurable link we can point to that clearly shows that students of music have a distinct advantage over their counterparts who are not participating in a music program.

There are fundamental, cornerstone reasons to include music as a part of the every child's curricular blueprint. When we stand back and take a holistic view, the value of music learning takes on an enriched perspective.

The study of music encourages:

Creativity. Creativity is the source of all possibilities. We are constantly challenged to explore this area of the mind. Music opens new horizons and new possibilities through expanded thinking. The study of music supports wonderment, imagination, appreciation, and sensitivity. Music allows us to experience creativity as an inventive thinking style.

Communication. Music is a language unto itself. Music can only be explained by music. If we do not expose our students to music, we are depriving them of an array of personal understandings that cannot be found in any other part of the school curriculum.

Critical Assessment. Intelligence is the ability to process facts and respond according to the given situation. Emotional stability stems from the capacity to deal with life's many inconsistencies. To accomplish both, the individual must be able to access the cognitive (analytical) and affective (emotional) sides of the mind. Music is one of the few academic disciplines that develops this ability and reinforces learning patterns to allow for greater critical assessment.

Commitment. Success is not measured by what we start but by what we complete. In music classes, students are required to perform the entire composition from beginning to end, to complete the given task. The important qualities of tenacity and persistence establish habits for positive, productive living that are applicable to every situation.

As teachers, we pledge our efforts to prepare our students for what lies ahead in their personal and professional journeys. In the process of preparing for a concert, sight reading new literature, teaching a musical concept, or listening to a high-quality performance, we help our students establish thinking habits that are immediately transferable to other academic areas. We are teaching the life skills that will support their healthy and prosperous futures.

It is apparent that the ongoing research spotlighting the benefits of music learning will continue to confirm what we have long suspected: *Music does make the difference.* As music educators, you awaken your students to the one of the most beneficial learning experiences of their lives . . . which means *you make a difference.*

Chapter 7

Advocacy Begins with the Director: You

*Never doubt that a small group of thoughtful,
dedicated individuals can change the world;
indeed, it is the only thing that ever has.*

Music advocacy begins with the director; it begins with a complete *knowing and understanding* of the mission; it begins with you. As stated in all the MENC materials, "Just as there can be no music without learning; no education is complete without music." Herein lies the foundation of the music educator's professional mission statement: the belief/knowing that learning music is a part of every young person's birthright. It is easy to lose sight of this truth in the heat of performance deadlines; however, this truth is the basis of every action taken, a fundamental truth that determines the prosperity of every program from beginning to end. We must first be believers before we can ethically engage others in our quest. "Why music?" is not an unfair question, but one deserving of a clear, concise, easily understood answer.

PHILOSOPHICALLY

1. *Music is intrinsic,* and in every individual; it is connected to the human spirit and creative mind. We cannot duplicate

it through any other form of expression; we cannot quantify it. It exists for its own sake.

Intellectually

2. *Music opens the mind.* Ongoing brain research continues to link the development of learning skills with music. The breakthrough work of Dr. Gordon Shaw (University of California-Irvine) and his colleagues affirms every musician's inherent knowing, but (until now) not scientifically proven theory of access to higher levels of creativity in every form of learning based on musical understanding.

Educationally

3. *Music teaches more than music.* While these characteristics are not specifically tied to the study of music, they are a by-products of the process:

   a. The establishment of high achievement standards transferable to other academic subjects.
   b. Development of keen problem-solving patterns.
   c. Establishment collaborative teamwork habits through communication skills.
   d. Understanding flexible thinking and adapting the known to the unknown.
   e. Improvement of reading comprehension, motor proficiency, spatial awareness, and listening ability.
   f. Mastery of a given challenge while expanding the realm of understanding and pushing beyond self-inflicted limits (raising of personal standards).

g. Increasing self-esteem, self-confidence, and self-discipline.

GLOBALLY

4. *Music is the universal language.* The shrinking globe dictates the need for establishing relationships with every world culture. Cross-civilization communication continues to be at the forefront of our very existence. Music creates sensitive individuals dedicated to dispelling prejudices that jeopardize the harmony of mankind.

This is all well and good, but these considerations mean little to present-day programs unless disseminated in an intelligent, understandable fashion to parents, school officials, political decision-makers, and even the students themselves. There is more to this music learning experience than renting an instrument and participating in band; it is focused on the preparation of the individual for a life of personal success and happiness.

Chapter 8

Music for Every Child

The goal of music performance is not perfection,
but expression.

Yo-Yo Ma

The term "music advocacy" continues to be a key phrase for music educators throughout the country. Since the early 1990s, groundbreaking research has spotlighted the importance of music-learning for every child. Everyone from civic leaders to political candidates has jumped on the arts bandwagon shouting (and touting) the benefits of music/arts education. It has certainly awakened the public, shifted the thinking of many school administrators, and created a long-overdue conversation about the educational, economical, and emotional value of music as it relates to the development of the child, every child.

It seems ludicrous to "defend music in our schools," particularly to someone with a musical background. We know we are the product of our passionate argument, and we often continue our dialogue with those of our same ilk. If we want our thoughts and beliefs to reach the decision-makers, we may need to "frame the presentation" using a vocabulary that demonstrates the value of music in their language, in their forum, and supporting their agenda.

Schools, by design, are created to prepare young people to assume the responsibilities of adulthood and become positive contributors to society, literally to create a better world for their generation and generations-to-come. As our globe shrinks (via technology, travel, international relations, etc.), it is imperative that we understand and share our cultural differences in a peaceful fashion creating a planet of peaceful existence. Simply put, music is the universal language that enhances the awareness of others and supports the freedom of expressive differences; music encourages (even demands) creative thinking, self-expression, problem solving, and risk taking, and it requires a high level of cooperation regardless of the belief systems of the music-makers. Cooperation, as opposed to competition, becomes the gateway to a higher level of aesthetic awareness and group achievement.

Music makes the difference. It is built on a platform that requires students to work together for a common goal. Music is a subject of self-discovery; the learning pattern is both impressionistic and expressionistic. It is a place for everyone, from the most talented performer to the beginner; all skill levels are accommodated in music class. It crosses all socioeconomic borders; music is inclusive. Above all, it connects to the musician in a unique way, allowing the student/performer to witness and acknowledge his or her self-worth. This acknowledgement is yet another bridge to the understanding of one's unlimited potential.

Unfortunately we often tend to sidestep the value of music learning as it relates to anything other than "music for the sake of music." However, if we are truly music advocates, let us embrace all outreach benefits, especially when they are the "common denominators of reason" to those who are creating, designing, and implementing the curricular blueprints for our schools.

In the words of Rolf Jensen, director of the Copenhagen Institute for Future Studies, "We are in the twilight of a society based on data. As information and intelligence become the domain of computers, society will place a new value on the human ability that cannot be automated: EMOTION."

We are in the business of "making better people and making people better." While raising test scores is one means of accomplishing this goal, may I suggest that the experience of music making will afford the learner the opportunity to integrate the learned data in a meaningful way that makes life worth living. With that theme in mind let us pledge our efforts to the ongoing task of sharing the good news about the value of music for *every* child.

Chapter 9

Advocacy as a Key Component of Every Program

*In the end we shall all have had enough of
cynicism and humbug and we shall want to
live our lives more musically.*

Vincent van Gough

What is the role of music advocacy in relation to your curricular agenda? It is imperative we inform everyone (administrators, parents, colleagues, community leaders, etc.) concerning the importance of music for *every* child. We can no longer simply teach those who show up at our educational doorstep; we must create and implement an ongoing network highlighting the immeasurable benefits of music-learning.

Recruitment and retention are always at the forefront of the music director's list of professional priorities. Whether it means working closely with the beginning members or discovering new ways to challenge the veterans, the enroll-ment and continued participation of the young musicians becomes the primary component as it relates to the growth and development of a high-quality program. We now enjoy a library of positive data that convincingly supports the value of music in our schools; sharing this information is certain to promote music and add a significant forward momentum to a musical organization, as well as all facets of the arts. Ultimately, this value is the most potent tool for effective and efficient recruitment and retention because it focuses on the unique educational, intrinsic, and aesthetic advantages enjoyed by musicians of all ages.

We are fortunate to live in a nation that offers *music* as a class option within the daily schedule. This creates two scenarios:

1. Teach the students who choose music as part of their class load.
2. Actively advertise and market the merits of learning and performing music.

The latter choice will produce a harvest far greater than the "wait-'n-see" option. It will also create a new understanding and greater appreciation of music education for everyone, including those who may decide not to enroll; all will gain from your advocacy efforts.

Too often, we don't take an active role in music advocacy because there is no threat to our local school music program. Complacency can lull us into a state of contentment/denial that is certain to unknowingly become our Achilles' heel. Then, when the predictable cutbacks begin and music becomes a target for the sharpened budgetary pencil, we (in desperation) turn to music advocacy as the save-all answer to the present predicament; by then, it is too little, too late. At best, it is a quick fix and (most certainly) one that will not last.

Music advocacy must be an ongoing process. Rather than thinking of it as a way to "justify music in our schools," it must be seen as an avenue of ongoing communication with present music-makers, potential music-makers, music supporters, fellow faculty members, administrators, and *all* parents. Music advocacy is used to increase awareness of the benefits of music making as it relates to every aspect of life. For those who have strong music programs, it serves as an affirmative reminder of the strength music offers to the entire curriculum. And for those who are involved with a music program in the growth mode, the advocacy information is certain to awaken an enthusiasm that can initiate a new attitude about the importance of a high-quality music curriculum in every school.

Music advocacy is no longer a luxury or something we turn to in times of crisis; it is a critical aspect of every program's healthy future and certain longevity. If we genuinely care about the future of music in our schools, then we must plant the musical seeds of understanding with everyone from school administrators to local politicians. Ongoing research continues to point to *music* as one of the most powerful forces in the development of the human, from mind potential to physical wellness. Above all, there is no other language that can describe *music*. As music educators we are obliged to share this good news.

Chapter 10

Setting the Stage for the Future of Music

In order to allow ourselves to be creative, we have to relinquish control and overcome fear. Why? Because real creativity is life-altering. It threatens the status quo; it makes us see things differently. It brings about change, and we are terrified by change.

Madeline L'Engle

Music advocacy is a hot topic-of-discussion for administrators, parents, teachers, and everyone keenly interested in creating the most potent curriculum possible for today's students. Breakthrough research continues to point to the study of music as a key component to personal success. It is development in every facet of personal and professional life.

In the mid-1990s, the work of Dr. Gordon Shaw and Dr. Frances Rauscher (University of California-Irvine) drew the attention of the national media by showing the neurological impact of listening to music and performing music. Recently, studies have evidenced the health/wellness benefits enjoyed as a result of making music. The scientific world and the artistic community are working in tandem to explore the unlimited power of music as it relates to human development. More importantly, it is apparent that this is only the beginning of the good news to come.

What relevance does music advocacy have to your life? We all seek "betterment" in our lives, whether it is in our workplace, our schools, our communities, or our social environments; there is an innate desire for improvement. It is no accident that we find a strong correlation between the educational, economical, and emotional well being of individuals and the link to music participation. We now understand music is not reserved for a select group of talented individuals, but it is an expressive language available to all who are interested in listening, playing, singing, and creating music. Everyone is a candidate to enjoy the rewards of music.

The good news is there are extraordinary benefits of studying music. Now we must take action to get this compelling data to everyone. The following questions concerning a successful music advocacy plan are focuses for each of us.

1. *Who should we approach with this powerful data?*
   It is imperative we share the good news with as many people as possible; therein lies the secret to bringing more music makers to the forum. Anyone who is interested in the welfare of the human race is a candidate for the powerful information.

2. *How do we go about it?*
   Advocating anything requires a dedication to communication. Everything from newsletters to e-mail server lists can be an avenue of exchange. We can take advantage of every high-tech communication vehicle to accomplish the goal.

3. *What is the target market?*

In particular, the people who are responsible for curriculum and scheduling in our schools are crucial to the cause. These educators make decisions based on the information-at-hand. Here is our opportunity to enthusiastically focus their attention on the value of music-study as it applies to the growth and development of every child.

4. *Where do we find all the statistics and research?*
How do we get the latest findings?

There are several free services that constantly bring the current information to your attention. Most states have active coalitions; MENC (The National Association of Music Educators), NAMM (International Music Products Association), and NARAS (National Association of Recording Arts and Sciences) all are actively involved in the music advocacy movement. Ask any music retailer and they can guide you to the right sources.

5. *Do we ever get to the point where our music advocacy efforts are completed?*

It is easy to read the material and be convinced of the importance of music; however, the task of music advocacy outreach often falls to the bottom of the "to do" list. We need pragmatic tools, blueprints for success, and helpful suggestions we can immediately adapt to our present circumstances.

You need contacts to serve as sources for your music advocacy library of data. Your own life has been influenced by music;

that's why you are reading this book. You have firsthand knowledge of the value of music as it relates to every aspect of your lifestyle. You know the discipline of music has a direct translation to the disciplines required for a happy, healthy life. You understand the positive difference music has made in your life.

The next step is to bring this awareness to others, to give them the gift of music. All too often we find ourselves saying, "That's true, but I'm just one person, and I can't make a difference." This is simply not true; the fact of the matter is, we need as many "one persons" as we can get to accept the challenge and spread the good news. Perhaps music advocacy isn't as much "what we do" as it is "who we are." We don't just *believe* in the fundamental value of music, we *know* music is an essential element of humankind. We must join hands and tell the story so our children, our grandchildren, and generations to come will have music in their lives.

We are one of the few nations that has successfully integrated music education as a choice in the daily school curriculum; music is not just for the "chosen few," but we can embrace all students, communicating to them the intrinsic value of music. Music for the sake of music; there is no substitute, and without the understanding of the immeasurable benefits of music learning, music listening, and music making, many people simply will never tap that creative part of their artistic potential. We must educate to perpetuate the theme: music *for all.*

Chapter 11

How Do We Go About It?

Courage is what it takes to stand up and speak; courage is also what it takes to sit down and listen.

Winston Churchill

In our continuing chapters concerning music advocacy we have looked at the "big picture." The next step in building our advocacy success blueprint is how to go about creating, implementing, and integrating a viable music advocacy program. Unfortunately, people are often intimidated by this seemingly impossible challenge; however, it is a matter of simply taking advantage of the network of exchange that is already in place. We must create various ways to dovetail on the existing schedule, curriculum, and various program agendas.

Granted, it is all too easy to push this responsibility aside, particularly since we cannot identify immediate and measurable results from our efforts. Much like planting a flower bulb, the reward (the bloom) is not apparent until much later. Often we do not see the results of our investment of time and energy for many years, and even then it is difficult to link the outcome to the origin of the plan. Most of our music advocacy work is done in "good faith" with the hope it will benefit many in the tomorrows that lie ahead. *Now* is the time to take action; the opportunities are endless, and the potential is beyond measure.

Communication is the key. Advocacy, by definition, means to "voice" an opinion, idea, and/or thought, literally "to add one's voice to the conversation." We can do this in a number of ways by taking advantage of the extraordinary communication circuit that is a part of our daily lives. By reading through the following suggestions, you will begin to create your own list of possibilities, and with each success, more options will appear.

E-mail. The popularity of Internet communication points to e-mail exchange as an obvious first step. Create an ever-growing "list of candidates" who could benefit from reading the compelling information about music learning and music listening, etc. Make the messages short and sweet, and create a comfortable outreach frequency for your cyberspace news clips supporting music advocacy.

Performances. Concerts always involve concert programs; this is an opportunity to put advocacy data into print on the backs of the programs, inserts highlighting the value of music, registration cards, and suggestion forms to allow the audience to become more involved as music supporters. We must create a bridge of communication by asking people to become a valued member of "the mission."

Community organizations. Whether the Rotary Club, the Optimists, Chamber of Commerce, or any facet of the community, these groups are made up of the town leaders, the people who are vitally interested in the health and welfare of the local society. When they choose to "get on the music bandwagon," they influence others by their actions. Ask for the opportunity to address the membership of the organization, and put the information in their hands. Their support is crucial.

Churches. Our spiritual life is threaded with music, and it is often taken for granted. From the church organist to the congregation singing the concluding hymn, we have made music an essential element of our worship service. Here is yet another chance to share the good news. Adding a music advocacy note on the back of the church bulletin will assure readership from a new audience, a group that benefits in many ways from the talents and skills of musicians of all ages. And again, we have the chance to gain more people to be part of our music support family.

Local media. Newspapers, television, and radio programmers are always looking for information that will draw the ears and eyes of the public. Good news is worthy news, and we have an abundance of "great news" to bring to their doorstep. Develop a relationship with the various people in the news media. Invite them to concerts, and encourage interviews with students, graduates, music parents, and administrators. Once they become your allies, the media forum will become a popular billboard for music, reaching a large audience of potential supporters.

Political leaders. This is, without question, the most vital aspect of our music advocacy efforts. The politicians are the decision-makers; one stroke of the budgetary sharpened pencil can instantly destroy many years of musical excellence in your community. To ignore this crucial area of music advocacy is naïve. Political leaders can be music's "best friend"; but they must be informed, and we must serve as the messengers-of-music. Seek those in your community who "speak the language" of politics; engage the support of these individuals and begin an ongoing dialogue with the local, regional, and state politicians.

The above six suggestions merely offer a starting place for successful music advocacy; the list is of possibilities is infinite, and it is limited only by our imaginations. We all have a surplus of ideas, but we must take action on these ideas by assertively stepping forward to create active communication.

Chapter 12

Successful Music Advocacy:
Communication Is the Answer

*The important thing is this: To be able at any
moment to sacrifice what we are for what we
could become.*

Lao-Tzu

Educational reformation is a way of life in American society.
Politicians are eager to include education as a mainstay of
their campaign platforms. Teachers know the curricula must
be in constant transition to accommodate the ongoing
growth of modern technology. Parents are keenly aware of
the importance of the learning atmosphere and are eager to
see their children experience a positive learning culture. In
the midst of this evolution, music, as well as the other fine
arts, has come to the educational forefront, and our nation is
embracing the arts as a basic subject for every child.

In 1990, the Music Educators National Conference (MENC),
the National Association of Music Merchants (NAMM), and
the National Association of Recording Arts and Sciences, Inc.
(NARAS) joined forces in establishing the National Coalition
for Music Education. The first priority of the organization is

*to garner the support of people who are aware of the impor-
tance of music in our schools and begin a dialogue with
state, regional, and district officials to promote music education
and to avoid any kind of program reduction or omission
based on budgetary decisions.* The state and local coalitions
are effective if they have strong leadership and the inclusive
involvement of teachers, parents, administrators, and community
patrons. As with any organization, success is measured by
the strength of its membership.

Advocacy, by definition, means: 1. To push; 2. To bolster;
3. To further a cause. As teachers of music, band directors
often allow advocacy responsibilities to slip to the bottom of
the priority list. The daily responsibilities—ranging from selecting
repertoire for the upcoming solo-ensemble festival to
negotiating with the drama teacher for access to the concert
hall—take precedence over any formally designed program
of music advocacy. Directors contend that there simply is not
enough time, and yet it is ever apparent that the outstanding
band programs integrate advocacy in all aspects of the
organization. It is not viewed as a separate responsibility, but
is synthesized as part of the musical climate; it is a focused
commitment, an ongoing sharing of the value of music in the
growth of *every* child.

Granted, in years past most colleges did not include a class
in "advocacy" as a requisite to the completion of the music
degree. Even today, advocacy is often combined with a
general methods class or included as an amendment to a
preparatory class in student-teaching. The point is, many

directors are clearly aware of the need for advocacy but feel a great sense of inadequacy in creating, developing, and maintaining an ongoing advocacy agenda. As a result we are depriving the students, the parents, the school, the community, and ourselves of many benefits that add artistic richness to the musical experience. As with any template of educational growth, the greatest form of learning is *doing*. We can no longer point the finger of blame at anyone; it is time to take action, shift the paradigm, and eagerly include advocacy in our teaching philosophies. It is time *to do, to take action,* to become active music advocates.

Chapter 13

Communicating to the Right Audiences

If you limit your actions in life to things that nobody can possibly find fault with, you will not do much.

Lewis Carroll

The Students. The greatest stage for advocacy is the rehearsal room. Who needs to understand the value of music more than anyone? *The students.* It will be of little use to convince others if the students are not privy to the benefits of music as it relates to their development.

Speak to the students concerning music as an expressionistic language. School, for the most part, is *impressionistic*—an exercise in memorizing various bits of information in preparation for the test. However, music offers the opportunity to involve the heart and mind in a process of personal expression, to reach beyond the notes on the page. Encourage the connection of the students' inner thoughts to the music; constantly remind them of the need to "be the music" and not just "play the music." The zenith for any musician is *to be one with the music.* With proper instruction, this could easily happen at the beginning level of music learning with the first note, and it should. Advocacy, at the level of

73

students, is supporting their love of music and their desire to continue their journeys of self-exploration. Conversely, if the student associates band (orchestra, choir, etc.) with a negative connotation, then all other advocacy efforts are of little consequence. First and foremost, the students must sense the teacher's dedication to music as an art form.

The Parents. The parents are more than just a body of people who raise funds for additional equipment or meet monthly for an update on the ensemble's planned activities. The parents have a vested interest in the program, and the director, in turn, has a responsibility to create an open line of communication that serves as a busy network of exchange relating the valuable impact music has on every student. Caution: when the parents/boosters are only an avenue to financial gains, the participation will be meager. If, however, the parent organization embraces the educational worth of music, the allegiance will evidence a notable increase in membership and active involvement.

Communication is the answer. It must be frequent, sincere, selfless, and dedicated to the parents' greatest concern: *the welfare of their child.* With the arrival of e-mail, the Internet, Web pages, etc., communication to an unlimited number of people is available at the touch of a computer key. Communication is not a luxury; it is a necessity. There is an endless supply of positive data ready to be shared with the parents; the challenge is to offer it to them in a user-friendly format. *Communication is the answer* and the key to all successful advocacy efforts.

Constantly reinforce the importance of music aside from the obvious: playing the clarinet, marching in the local parade, or performing at the annual holiday concert are tangible measurements of music education, but we know these events only cover the tip of the iceberg. Remind the parents that music *builds critical thinking skills, prepares students for the rigors of higher education, invigorates the process of learning, and pushes the mind to an advanced level of competence.* The excitement of the concert will be short lived, but the awareness of the long-range advantages of music education will serve as a strong influence for future parental decision making.

The Administrators. Administrators, in almost every case, are former classroom teachers. They made a career choice to contribute to the education of children by assuming a set of new challenges. Like everyone, their administrative choices are based on available information. With rare exceptions, the administrator will do what is best (in his or her perception) for the positive educational growth and development of the students. To assume the administrator is aware of the benefits of music education is professional naiveté. In many cases the principal, supervisor, superintendent, etc. only sees/evaluates the results of the music classes at a basketball game (the pep band), at graduation (the band without seniors), or the Fourth of July parade (summer band with the new eighth graders). This is hardly a fair assessment of a teacher's academic worth. In many instances, the music wing of the school is at the opposite end of the building; administrators and directors can go weeks, even months, without seeing one another. This creates, by proximity, a void in communication. Remember: *communication is the answer.*

Paying frequent visits to the administrator's office offering important music information is as vital as tuning the band before the rehearsal begins. Inviting the administrators to come to class (rehearsal) is always an eye-opening experience for all. Student leaders can serve as messengers of good news concerning the program by requesting monthly update meetings with administrators. Parents should be encouraged to seek various ways to include administrators in the booster meetings and events. Create a partnership with the administrator and the music program; by doing so, the administrator becomes a music advocate via the inclusion process.

The Colleagues. The word "colleague" generally refers to music colleagues. Consider other teachers in the school as your advocate-colleagues. Humans are infamous for polarizing with their own ilk or likeness, and education is no exception; English teachers talk to one another, coaches stick together, elementary educators chat with other elementary teachers, and music educators are no different. It is not easy to garner the support of interdisciplinary colleagues if we only communicate with other music educators. Advocacy is based on outreach. It is difficult to convince anyone of anything if we wait for people to come to us. We cannot afford to idly sit in the music office hoping others will have a sudden artistic revelation. When a music teacher says, "There isn't enough time to get to know the other teachers in the school," it demonstrates a shortsightedness that builds a certain communication barrier. In truth we must know *every* teacher in the school; these colleagues are key members of the advocacy team.

More than 30 percent of college graduates participated in their high school music programs. One could easily conclude that one out of every three teachers in the school has participated in band, orchestra, or choir. It is time to *bring them back to music,* and they will become new advocate-leaders for other faculty members. Invite your colleagues to play in a concert, work with a sectional, travel with the ensemble, be a soloist at a concert, serve as the announcer, become part of the music program. The dormant but enthusiastic adult musician is simply waiting for an opportunity to rejoin the band. It is very likely that one-third of the school faculty are already music advocates; tap this powerful source of support.

The Community Leaders. It is true: *if the quality of student education diminishes, the community's lifestyle will also diminish.* The Athenians were well aware of the crucial balance between education and community welfare. (Music was also a required subject in the Greek educational system.) Our forefathers insisted on an education for every child (represented by our public schools) for they knew it would secure America's position as a world leader. This theme is evident at the national, state, regional, and local levels. In smaller communities, the music teacher is the focal point of arts education, and the people of the community look to this individual (you) for advice, direction, and all expertise dealing with music. They must be included in the communication loop; otherwise they will assume music education is what they hear on the radio and see on television. These people are taxpayers, voters, members and friends of the Board of Education, golfing partners with your administrators, and colleagues. The conversations they have with their friends and acquaintances must positively support music education, and the most persuasive voice in the community is the music director's.

The opportunities for community participation are endless, literally at the limits of the imagination, but the thoughts must be directed to mine the gems hidden within the local population. Does the editor of the area newspaper play trombone? Is the grocery store owner a percussionist? Did your doctor, minister, insurance agent sing in a choir? Even if they do not want to perform, rest assured they will want to contribute in some fashion, for they know the value of a solid music education. Reach out to them, and invite them to be active members of your advocacy organization; they will eagerly join.

Most successful business people are eager to support education. They realize their own achievements are a product of their knowing, their education. You can count on them for financial contributions if you can demonstrate through advocacy what their help will mean to the youth of the community. Do not expect the potential philanthropists to seek out the music program; you must go to them. It is the responsibility of the music advocate to make the first move. *Communication is the answer.*

The General Public. Contrary to popular thought, the general public is very much in favor of music education. The overwhelming opinion of the American people is very pro-music, pro-art. Karl Bruhn, former director of market development for the National Association of Music Merchants, was a key figure in the establishment and organization of the National Coalition. In one of his many essays, "On Preaching to the Choir: The Good News and the Bad News," he states (in reference to the 1992 Harris poll prepared at the request of the American Council for the Arts): *"More than nine out of ten polled, for example, said it was important for children to learn about the arts and to develop artistic interests in school."* He goes on to say:

> What the results of the Harris poll really mean is that we have to redouble our efforts to make sure the right message gets to the right people. We have to tell the decision makers not just that education in music and other arts has intrinsic value, or that it is the "right thing to do," but this is what the people in their community and in their state—in large numbers—want their children to learn.

Much of the groundwork is in place for advocacy; the missing link to the puzzle appears to be leadership at the local level. Advocacy begins with the music educator. While it is possible to delegate individual duties along the way, the advocacy wellspring is, and will always be, part of the mission of every music teacher. There is an army of support ready and eager to come forward that is already convinced that the arts/music have a place in the educational framework of our youth. Take the lead: become the focal point for pro-music advocacy within your community.

Chapter 14

Accessing the Information Sources

The greatest discovery of my generation is that human beings can alter their lives by altering their attitudes of mind.

William James

Music advocacy is not a complicated agenda requiring extensive research and the ability to quote lofty phrases or to speak in platitudes. On the contrary, it is the chance to share the wonderful awareness that music makers enjoy a better life. While the message seems simplistic, it is confirmed time and time again, and it is the fundamental theme of all music advocacy.

Herein lies the "meat and potatoes" of our mission, the substantive facts and figures that clearly demonstrate the positive life-benefits gained through music education. It represents the very foundation of our cause.

We have focused on:

- Those we need to approach with the powerful data.
- How we go about creating a template of effective communication.
- What constitutes the target market and how to have the greatest impact.

Now we spotlight the all-important sources of the latest research statistics.

[**Author's note:** In truth we have an abundance of convincing data to support the theme: "Every student in the nation should have an education in the arts." The challenge is to sift through the mountain of scientific evidence to clearly state our case in a powerful and concise fashion and in a language that is understood by everyone. It is easy to become lost in the extensive library of facts and figures; therefore, this chapter offers a certain recipe for advocacy success and, at the same time, creates a network to access the information yet to come.]

The most potent all-in-one advocacy tool is "The Music Education Advocacy Kit" (commonly referred to as "The Einstein Kit") produced by NAMM (The International Music Products Association) and VH1 Save the Music. The kit includes:

The Music Advocate's Guide, a packet of brochures high-lighting irrefutable facts about the benefits of music instruction. The colorful handout is packed with compelling data taken from research-findings around the globe, including the titles:

"Piano Raises Conceptual Math Scores"
"Music Students Score Higher SATs"
"Second Graders Do Sixth Grade Math"
"Music Makes the Brain Grow"
"Rhythm Students Learn Fractions Better"

Advocate's Toolkit CD-ROM, a treasury of materials featuring a complete school board presentation in PowerPoint, press releases, fact sheets, research summaries, and a selection of public-service radio announcements featuring musical artists speaking about the power of music in their lives. There is also a series of sample letters to community leaders, administrators, Board of Education members, etc.

Music and the Mind Video, a composite of nationally televised news clips from various educators, scientists, journalists, artists, and students. The video is a perfect vehicle to share the "benefits of music" with the decision-makers in the school community. For further information about "The Einstein Kit" contact NAMM at 1-800-767-6266.

MENC (The National Association for Music Education) has an extensive library of advocacy materials, including various action kits, videos, brochures, reprinted articles, etc. The organization's mission is to ensure that every child has the opportunity to enjoy a balanced, sequential, high-quality education including music as a core subject. The MENC Web site offers a wide array of ready-to-share publications and cyberspace links to other advocacy avenues at www.menc.org, or 703-860-4000. You will find the MENC family of educators eager to extend a helping hand and join with you in your music advocacy goals.

Internet users may take advantage of WhyMusicEd@aol.com. This free e-mail service generates weekly messages that can be downloaded and added to your advocacy materials. It is an ongoing service that accommodates several thousand music education supporters around the world. WhyMusicEd also is a source for *all* materials used to support music in our schools (1-800-332-2637).

VH1 Save the Music is a not-for-profit foundation supported by the VH1 cable network and its partners. Of their many contributions, including an extensive instrument donation program to establish school music programs to schools without them, the organization sponsors national public service announcements promoting the advantages of music education. The VH1 Save the Music staff members are dedicated music advocates eager and willing to work with all who are committed to the welfare of music education. You may call 1-888-841-4687 or access their extensive Web site, www.vh1.com.

Finally, **The American Music Conference** is a non-profit educational association that promotes the importance of music, music making, and music education to the general public. AMC's Web site contains links to national standards for music education, research information on music-learning, and other music related topics at www.amc-music.com. You can also reach AMC at 760-431-9124.

As you can quickly tell, there is no lack of information or information resources to support the immeasurable benefits of music learning. We need to create allies in our local communities and school systems who comprehend the implications of music study and who also understand there can be no true education without proper training in the arts. We have an incredible opportunity to enlighten everyone, and with it goes the responsibility to manifest this opportunity for the welfare of today's youth and all those to be educated in the future. To this end, let us pledge our efforts and energies. The results will be shared by all.

PART THREE
*The Selection and Development
of Effective Student Leaders*

Chapter 15

Character Traits of a Student Leader

A leader is best when people barely know he exists,
Not so good when people obey and acclaim him,
Worse when they despise him.
Fail to honor people, they will fail to honor you;
Of a good leader, who talks little:
When his work is done, his aim fulfilled,
They will say, "We did this all ourselves."

Lao-Tzu

Student leaders are no longer a luxury in our educational world, but a necessity, particularly in the field of music. Any successful ensemble is made up of a strong director and a committed group of responsible and dedicated student leaders. We count on these extraordinary young people to offer their time and energy in the ongoing growth and development of our programs; without them, much daily work simply would not be completed.

Students are usually eager to assume leadership roles, but are they capable of assuming the responsibilities that accompany the real leadership agenda? Do they truly understand the personal price of leadership? The selection process cannot be taken lightly, for the student leaders will often determine the attitude, the atmosphere, and the level of achievement for the entire organization; they are the pace-setters for every member of the ensemble.

So many factors enter into this important choice. Are the candidates competent? Are they emotionally secure? Will they assume a leadership posture both in and out of the rehearsal environment? Can they handle stress and pressure? Are they willing to make decisions that are not self-serving but focused on their followers? Do they accept criticism and learn from their mistakes? Are they selfless rather than selfish? Ultimately, will they serve as positive role models for each and every band student? These are not easy questions to answer, but they are crucially important inquisitions, for it is unfair to everyone to assign leadership responsibilities to an individual who has not developed the level of maturity needed to assume the added responsibilities associated with productive leadership.

Over the years of teaching the skills and techniques of student leadership, I have observed so many students who are confident in their abilities and certain they can "do the job" and do it quite well; however, they have great difficulty turning hopes and visions into reality. The results are devastating to their followers, the program, and the perceived self-worth of the leader. In truth, everyone loses. How can we, as directors, avoid this dilemma?

In our urgency to have our students become more responsible and productive (perhaps these are one in the same), we are constantly looking for those opportunities of growth that will allow them to experience the pathway to success. After all, our fundamental mission as educators is to prepare students for the rigors of adulthood. It is exciting and personally gratifying when we see students rise to the occasion, but the penalty of failure has a high price tag in terms of the emotional damage to a student's self-concept. Unlike many other aspects of education, failure in student leadership means others feel the effects of the shortcoming. If a student leader does not accomplish the given task, it can (and often does) have a negative impact on all the followers, and the consequences can range from outward hostility to exclusion from the group. In extreme cases, the wounded student leaders will make a decision never to be put in a similar situation where they will be subject to such personal pain.

Metaphorically, we do not pick a tomato from a garden until it is ripe, for it will be of no value to anyone. It is impossible to place the prematurely picked vegetable back on the mother plant. Likewise, a student leader who is not ready (unripe) will be incapable of surviving the pressure and stress of leadership if he or she has not grown to the necessary stage of leadership maturity. There is an art to the selection process, and veteran educators are careful to find the students who are:

- **Selfless.** Watch for the students who are always taking the time to help those around them. You can quickly identify this important trait—consideration for others—by simply observing student behavior before and after rehearsals.

- **Persistent.** Tenacity is an attribute necessary for attaining excellence at any discipline. Many people will begin a new endeavor with a sense of positive enthusiasm, but you are interested in the students who "complete" their assigned responsibilities. We are not measured by what we begin but by what we complete.

- **Consistent.** Most student leaders are at a time in their lives when they are establishing their personal habits and their life values; they are truly deciding "who they are." Dreams, goals, and desires can shift radically from one day to the next. Pinpoint the students who are predictable and demonstrate emotional stability, those who can "stay the course."

- **Affable.** It is often tempting to favor the student leader who is a gifted musician, and this is certainly an important aspect of his or her qualifications; however, it is vital for the student leader to have a healthy rapport with the other members of the organization. Popularity aside, the chosen student leader must be recognized and respected by the majority of the group.

- **Honest.** Slighting the truth is commonplace. The student who avoids the temptation to exaggerate or embellish the truth and is willing to accept the consequences that often accompany honesty is a rare commodity. Everyone will benefit from being in the presence of a person who demonstrates such personal integrity.

- **Faithful and Loyal.** "United we stand, divided we fall." This well-worn phrase is still classic advice for every leader. The students who are always tried-and-true loyalists are your best nominees for student leadership positions. At this stage of leadership, commitment to the group is mandatory and any disagreements or issues should be dealt with behind closed doors and in strict confidentiality.

These six personality traits are only a starting point; however, they will establish a strong foundation for the selection and qualification of any student leader. We, as educators, must be sensitive to the overwhelming effects student leadership can have on the development of the individual. We are in a position to help our students create a sense of self-worth that will serve them throughout their lives. We can guide their efforts and energies to ensure a positive experience for all concerned. As their leaders, we have an immeasurable influence on their leadership for life.

Chapter 16

A Paradigm Shift for Today's Leaders

Blessed are those who can give without remembering and take without forgetting.

Elizabeth Bibesco

The entire realm of leadership training has taken a dramatic shift over the past three decades or so. The strong-armed approach to leadership success has given way to the concept of allowing the follower to become an invested contributor to the overall mission. There is a greater emphasis on intrinsic motivation rather than using extrinsic rewards as a means to individual or group achievement.

The cornerstones of this paradigm shift emphasize a win-win concept embracing both the requirements of the project responsibilities and the welfare of the people involved. It diminishes the power struggle often associated with the traditional positioning, turf protection, rank-and-file status, etc. To find success in this modern-day blueprint of leadership style, these four laws of leadership must be understood and integrated into every decision made by the assigned leader; they serve as the foundation blocks of contemporary leadership.

People are more important than titles. The focal point remains on the welfare of the people involved. The leader constantly monitors the overall attitude of the group, ensuring a sense of mutual understanding and synergistic effort based on individual and group commitment to focus on the agreed objectives.

We can't lead others until we lead ourselves. Role modeling plays a vital part in the leader's ongoing communication with the members of the organization. While delegation is still an important aspect of the process, the leader sets the pace by demonstrating the expectations and the standards desired to achieve positive results. The most effective form of leadership is positive role modeling.

Leaders are measured by what they give. Leadership is an opportunity "to give" to those who are part of the group, organization, or ensemble. The position of leadership is a license to help all those who are part of the forum. If there is not a measured contribution to the forward progress of the group, the value of the leader is diminished to the point of being "merely a title carrier."

Leaders assume total responsibility. When something goes awry, the leader immediately assumes the responsibility for the breakdown rather than pointing the finger of blame at anyone else. The welfare of the followers is primary in every facet of the leader's agenda.

Adapting this new leadership consciousness to any musical ensemble offers the individual players a greater opportunity to "own the group" and accept the responsibilities for the positive growth and development of the organization. Everyone wins.

Chapter 17

The Personal Values of a Student Leader

*It is one of the beautiful compensations of this
life that no one can sincerely try to help another
without helping oneself.*

Charles Dudley Warner

When asked who would like to serve in a leadership role in
the music program, do the students really comprehend the
extended effort and energy required to fulfill the responsibilities
and agendas that lie ahead?

All too often an enthusiastic, young want-to-be leader will
eagerly assume the coveted title only to be quickly disillusioned
following several unsuccessful attempts to garner group
support while trying to accomplish the given project.
Personal discouragement leads to "giving up," and (unfortunately) all future leadership opportunities are avoided based
on past experiences of perceived failure.

Do we properly prepare our students for "what lies ahead"
when they choose to become student leaders? Or do we simply
(and randomly) pick this or that person to fill the given position?
Are your leaders selected via a popularity vote, or are they
chosen because of their abilities, skills, talents, and intentions?

93

Leadership is made up of two philosophical components:

1. Leadership is for *giving.*
2. Leadership is *forgiving.*

Many young people see a leadership position as the chance to be in charge, to tell others what to do, to delegate work, and to put themselves in a posture of authority. Nothing could be further from the truth. The essence of an effective leader lies in the student's ability to serve others, to create success for the people in the organization. It is the opportunity to give, to contribute, to roll up one's sleeves and begin moving in a positive, forward direction. Whether it is straightening the chairs, putting the stands away, creating a colorful bulletin board, or working with someone on a musical passage, the leader is the person who does the task at hand. A leader does "what needs to be done, when it needs to be done, whether he or she wants to do it or not, without anybody asking."

The second aspect of leadership centers on the concept of forgiving. When something goes awry (and it will), many young leaders want to react to the situation by reprimanding the followers for their inability to fulfill the leaders' suggestions. However, the true leader will forgive the people involved and proactively refocus his or her energies to correct the problem and quickly get back on course. Psychologically (and intellectually) we know that people do not get better by making them feel worse.

All too often, there is a tendency for young leaders to chastise those who fall short on the given assignment; nothing could be more detrimental to the trusting relationship necessary for future success in any leader/follower relationship. The solution is simple: forgive, correct, and proceed forward.

When selecting students who will be working with their peers in a leadership capacity, look beyond their group popularity, their musical gifts, and even their academic standing. Observe how they interact with others, and pay special attention to those who always are considerate of their fellow students and willing to serve them by going above and beyond the call of duty. These are the candidates who are most likely to succeed as leaders; they "live" the values required of every contributing leader by **giving** and **forgiving.**

Chapter 18

Choosing Leaders:
Maturity Is the Key

*Growth is the process of responding positively
to change. Grappling with hardships, trouble,
and calamity; facing adversity in a spirit of
determination and courage; loving and not
being crushed by broken hopes; holding our
heads up high, having done our best . . .
this is growth.*

- How do you choose your student leaders?

- Are there specific criteria to use in the selection of these crucially important role models?

- Do you have a particular standard they must achieve before they are candidates?

- What are the expectations you have of these people?

After studying and working with countless student leaders over the years, it is clearly apparent that some students are ready for the extra responsibility student leadership requires, and many are not. What determines this crucial difference? It appears to lie in the area of individual maturity—not chronological age, but personal maturity. Some young folks easily assume (and consume) the added workload, while others may buckle under the pressure. As teachers, we have an obligation to be sensitive in our selection of student leaders, for we are asking these individuals to give up the privileges of their classmates and enter into a role that will demand their undivided attention if they are to succeed. As you can quickly see, being a student leader requires an individual to give up much of his or her freedom in return for the opportunity to dedicate more time and energy to the given goal.

While being a student leader is often misinterpreted as a status upgrade, it is in truth the acquisition of more responsibilities. It is all too easy for the aspiring student leader to be blinded by the enthusiasm of the moment and accept the charge before truly understanding what will be required of him or her. This is where we, as caring educators, must be cautious and realistic in our assessment of a student's "readiness." Once again, let us revisit the original questions pertaining to the selection process; it is imperative that we begin with this inquiry: Is the student mature enough to emotionally embrace the task(s) at hand in a fashion that will positively add to his or her personal growth and development? Simply put, can the student handle what will be asked? Although there is no definitive template to measure something as arbitrary as maturity, there are some general guidelines that can help you in identifying those students who are being considered for student leadership positions.

Levels of Maturity

Level I: Selfish–Selfishness focuses on the preoccupation with "self." Even students who are steller musicians can easily become upset unless everything supports their welfare and opinion. Beware the student who unconsciously, or by design, makes decisions that support his or her self-promotion and/or personal agenda. Little will be gained if he or she is given the power to make decisions that will impact others. Inevitably, more time will be spent dealing with the problems caused by immature decision making than will be spent enjoying the benefits of the young leader's efforts. We often rationalize the fact that these students might, in fact, prosper by putting them "up front" or giving them extra responsibilities. Alas, it is rare that they will rise to the occasion. It would be a much kinder and more positive choice to allow them to spend extra time in the growth process before asking them to put others' considerations and personal welfare ahead of their own.

Level II: Independent–We often see "independence" as a reaction to the lack of results achieved with a "selfish" attitude. The human mind comes up with a logical reason why others do not respond to our wishes and concludes, "It is easier to just do it myself than to depend on others and be disappointed." Many people function at this level throughout life and are quite successful; however, they are unto themselves and perfectly satisfied to "do their own thing." In fact, they may be uncomfortable letting others get involved. Since they produce excellence in their area of interest, we are often deluded into thinking they will transfer a similar standard of achievement to their followers. When given a leadership position, however, the "independent" may become frustrated when the followers do not immediately choose to replicate his or her personal habits and work patterns. These individuals have a tendency to give up in disgust when the going gets rough and revert to the "I'll just do it myself" habit that has served them so well in the past.

Level III: Cooperative–A student must be at Maturity Level III (Cooperative) before being considered for any kind of leadership position that involves dealing with other people. Cooperative personalities are aware that nothing will be gained without a sense of mutual understanding and that all this must be well fueled with a cooperative attitude. Then, and only then, the I–me syndrome gives way to a genuine we–us approach to every situation. Satisfying the ego will become secondary to the forward motion and the personal welfare of the group. This student leader understands that the benefits of cooperative decision making are far greater than self-serving independent choices. Granted, it takes a mature individual to see beyond the instant gratification derived from serving oneself before thinking of others. Level III, Cooperative, is a transition to the final and most important perspective needed for effective leadership.

Level IV: Giving–We have many examples of "givers," and we all know those who will go the extra mile, but this level of "giving" does not require any kind of reciprocation. Those who operate from a posture of "giving" do so for the pleasure of the process. The payoff for this individual lies totally in the opportunity to serve. While a "thank you" is appreciated, it is not required. The payment lies in the process of the giving. So often student leaders will find themselves discouraged because nobody recognizes their dedicated efforts. It is true we all enjoy personal acknowledgement along the pathway of life, but a mature leader is clearly aware that the most important affirmation of his or her leadership success is often disguised in the extension of more work and extra responsibilities being added to the leadership agenda. In essence, "The reward for a job well done is the opportunity to do more." The student leader who is a genuine "giver" is a rare commodity; everyone in the group will gain by experiencing the magic created by a giving leader. It is his or her presence that makes the difference. What greater role model could there possibly be for the followers?

The student leader selection process is certain to affect every aspect of your program. All too often we make our choices based on everything from age and talent level to attendance and personality. In all fairness to everyone, we must be honest in assessing the maturity of those students who want to be given the opportunity to serve others through various student leadership positions. Carefully seek the student who wants to improve the conditions for his or her compatriots by unselfishly contributing to the given goal. When you find this individual, you have identified a student leader in action. Put this individual in charge; let this student take the lead.

Chapter 19

Solution-Driven Leaders:
The Ultimate Choice

To be a genuine individualist requires a great deal of strength and courage. It is never easy to chart new territory, to cross new frontiers, or to introduce subtle shadings to an established color.

Toller Cranston

How many times have we heard the phrase "You are either part of the problem or you are part of the solution"? In choosing our student leaders, it is vitally important to select exemplary role models who are *solution-oriented,* rather than *problem-plagued.*

Students who wish to serve in a leadership capacity must first understand that true leadership requires an individual to do more than his or her counterparts; it is about serving others. Student leaders are the doers; they are the people who roll up their sleeves and go to work.

Even after an extensive explanation of the personal and group expectations, I often wonder if the hopeful student leader really understands the level of commitment, dedication, patience, and personal sacrifice. For those students who wish to take on the challenges of leadership, and for those directors who are looking for the student who has the right leadership qualifications, review the following.

Focus on the solution, not the problem. A gifted leader will seek an objective/solution and then begin to move in the direction of the given goal, rather than dwelling on the current status and all the reasons the organization cannot reach the objective. This comes about by using a clear and concise blueprint of a *solution-driven* vs. a *problem-driven* plan of action.

The solution-driven leader spotlights the strengths of the followers and emphasizes what is already working. Instead of quickly pointing out everything that is wrong, ineffective, inefficient, and preventing forward progress, the leader will first make a point to recognize the various aspects of the project (including the people) that give it credibility and make it worth the follower's investment of time and energy. The benefit package must be obvious, or there will be no ownership of responsibility by the followers and, thus, no group cooperation and lackluster participation.

The solution-driven leader sets a stage of open communication and personal involvement. Too often we look for those we can blame for the present predicaments; such behavior can garner initial agreement and emotional approval, but it has nothing to do with solving the problem. It is, at best, a momentary "feel good" and rarely serves the group or the leader. This leader will create a safe, open forum of communication with everyone and listen to any and all suggestions in an effort to attain a better outcome; in turn, everyone begins to become more involved in the implementation of a plan that reflects the group's thoughts and ideas.

The solution-driven leader keeps everyone focused on the goal. We often sabotage ourselves by dwelling on the opposite of what we want. Noted psychologist/philosopher Abraham Maslow said, "The mind will lead us in the direction of its dominant thought." If we spend our time thinking about why something will not work, we are leading ourselves to a predictable failure. A solution-driven leader will continue to communicate the desired goal to the members of the group; what the mind can conceive, the person can achieve. We must picture high-level achievement in our minds at all times and be realistic in the assessment of what it will take to reach the goal. This is one of the fundamental responsibilities of every student leader; focus the energy of the followers on the anticipated results.

The solution-driven leader creates energy and enthusiasm. The best way a leader can create energy and enthusiasm for a group is to model positive energy and sincere enthusiasm. This does not necessarily mean assuming the role of a cheerleader or extending shallow, insincere compliments. It merely means demonstrating a genuine care for the people, the goal, and the welfare of everyone involved. A lethargic, negative leader will drain energy from any group. This leader will amplify the problems facing the organization; on the other hand, an enthusiastic, positive leader will infuse the group with the needed energy to move forward and discover the endless possibilities available as a result of group cooperation. The solution-driven leader understands the secret to all leadership, the one aspect over which he or she has complete control in every situation: *the ability to choose one's attitude at every moment of every day.*

The solution-driven leader creates an atmosphere conducive to effective and efficient problem solving while giving continuous renewal to everyone involved. Being a leader does not mean "having all the answers." Young leaders often think they are responsible for every solution, answer, and resolution; such logic can result in frustration, confusion, and even delusion. A perceptive and effective leader will encourage an ongoing exchange of helpful ideas from those who are part of the group. Every suggestion will be met with genuine appreciation, and the communication will be used as an opportunity to confirm the value of the person involved. (If we inadvertently or purposefully reject someone's suggestions, we stifle his or her creativity and construct a barrier preventing further communication.) Maintaining an open, honest, safe environment for group problem solving is seen by many as the most important contribution of any solution-driven leader.

Young people are often enamored by the "idea" of leadership and the personal benefits they perceive to be a part of the leadership position. Choose those who can comprehend the "reality" of leadership, those who are willing to go the extra mile on behalf of their peers. Choose those who understand that the key to quality is the collective work ethic of their followers.

Chapter 20

Does Your Group C.A.R.E?

*You cannot do a kindness too soon because
you never know how soon it will be
too late.*
Kindness in words creates confidence.
Kindness in thinking creates profoundness.
Kindness in giving creates love.

Lao-Tzu

What makes a musical ensemble special? What creates that magical atmosphere we have come to know as the foundation of a musical family? Perhaps it is all based on the ability to C.A.R.E. If one examines the common themes of great music programs, the best organizations always focus on the C.A.R.E. of their fellow members, their directors, and all those connected with the music program. Does your group C.A.R.E.?

The acronym is more than a clever label; it is the essence of why any group becomes successful. It is the elusive indescribable climate we all recognize, but often overlook in our quest for quality. This acronym provides the forum we all need to achieve a high level of musical excellence.

To C.A.R.E. means:

Communication: Is there open and safe communication among the members of the group? Do the upperclassmen spend time with the new members? Do various sections of the ensemble work together with a unified understanding? We know communication is the key to all forward motion and problem resolution. Encourage one another to reach out to other members of the group; harmony and balance apply to more than great music making.

Attitude: What kind of attitude do the group members generate? Do people look forward to the time together in an environment based on positive support and encouragement? Since every individual has total control over his or her attitude, this may be the most important area of personal contribution to the musical family. There is no substitute for a healthy attitude; it is as important as good intonation.

Responsibility: The word literally means "the ability to respond." Do people seriously embrace their responsibilities? Do they come to rehearsals ready to invest their efforts and energies for the ongoing growth and development of the ensemble's goals? Do they understand their personal contribution (both positive and negative) plays a crucial role in the outcome of the ensemble's success? Does the group respond to the director in a fashion that will advance the entire organization to the next level of artistry?

Excellence: Is "excellence" the key word for everything connected with the program? Excellence is the by-product of seeking quality, and quality can be applied to every aspect of life. Whether it is putting away music after a practice, straightening the rehearsal room, or practicing scales, all of these (plus every other action) need to reflect a sense of excellence, to "excel," to go beyond the requirements, to put forth the extra effort.

The veteran ensemble people know "the feel" of a group that *cares*. We can buy all the right instruments, build a great rehearsal building with all the latest high-tech equipment, get access to a huge music budget, purchase the finest music available, and surround the group with wonderful teachers, but the secret ingredient comes from within the group: the ability to C.A.R.E.

Don't chase the dream by going on trips, buying new equipment, or even by changing music directors; you will be sorely disappointed. The answer lies within the members of the ensemble. When the people *in a musical group* decide to unselfishly *give to the musical group,* it's then that we realize the value *of the ensemble,* a gathering of wonderful young musicians who genuinely C.A.R.E. for one another.

PART FOUR
The Band Director as a Leader

Chapter 21

The Art of Music and the Art of Teaching

Life is a lot like jazz . . . it's best when you improvise.

George Gershwin

In today's educational system, the band director is far more than a trained musician capable of conducting an array of beat patterns. Most of his or her school day is dedicated to a host of other responsibilities, and the much-cherished podium time is all too brief; therefore, it is crucial to make use of every moment spent *rehearsing the band.* Time lost during rehearsals is lost forever, and the negative results of wasted time far exceed what is casually observed. Students often become frustrated and discouraged, and most rehearsals become an unpleasant experience rather than "the best time of the day."

The band director is in a position to organize and lead students to new levels of musical understanding and expression. It is clear that the band director must be a leader of people as well as a conductor of music. Blending both of these important aspects of teaching into one personality ensures a successful rehearsal for everyone involved. We cannot ignore the leadership attributes of the band director, but must emphasize them in ongoing professional development.

Traditionally, our colleges and universities do not require classes in the area of "people skills." It has always been assumed that a solid library of musical knowledge would suffice in the development of a successful teacher. In defense of these institutions of higher learning, there is little if any time for elective courses if one is to complete the mandated requirements in a strict degree program.

Additional classes outside the discipline of music are next to impossible. With the present requisites, many students need five years to complete and receive their undergraduate diploma. In spite of this, we must take note of ongoing research that specifically demonstrates the vital importance of various personality traits in determining success in the rehearsal classroom.

Chapter 22

Personality Traits Needed for Success

The mediocre teacher tells.
The good teacher explains.
The superior teacher demonstrates.
The great teacher inspires.

William Arthur Ward

In the ERIC document *Characteristics of Effective Music Teachers* (University of Houston, no. ED 237 400), Dr. Manny Brand reports, "Although possession of a high of degree of musicianship was assumed, there are other essential qualities that a band director must possess."

1. Enthusiasm.
2. Warmth and personal interest.
3. A rehearsal technique combining clarity, brevity, fast pace, and variety.
4. A balance of praise and meaningful criticism.
5. A discipline technique focusing on communication.
6. A desire to improve and learn.

In a sequel to this study, Brand concludes, *The ingredients of a master music teacher are: a sixth sense of understanding his or her students, pride in his or her remarkable competence, a fertile imagination, a theatrical flair, instructional urgency, a drive to accomplish the highest musical goals, [and] the drive to work hard and obtain enormous satisfaction.*

Clearly, this spotlights the band director as a teacher and communicator as well as a musician.

Mike Manthei of Valley City State University, Valley City, North Dakota, cowrote "A Preliminary Investigation into the Qualities of a Successful Band Director" with Ray Roth of Mackinaw City, Michigan, as part of the abstract sponsored by *The American School Band Directors Association*. The two men reached a similar conclusion to Brand's. Quoting P. B. Baker's research, "The Development of a Music Teacher Checklist for Use by Administrators, Music Supervisors, and Teachers Evaluating Music Teaching," the ten most important characteristics of a successful music teacher/band director are:

1. Enthusiasm for teaching and caring for students.
2. Strong but fair discipline.
3. Observable student enjoyment, interest, and participation.
4. Communication skills.
5. Sense of humor.
6. In-depth musicianship.
7. Knowledge and use of good literature.
8. Strong rapport with the students, both individually and as a whole.
9. High professional standards.
10. The use of positive group management techniques.

Manthei and Roth also bring the work of T. C. Saunders and J. L. Worthington ("Teacher Effectiveness in the Performance Classroom." *Update.* 8 (2) 26-29.) to their document with the revealing discovery that (aside from the high level of musical competencies) the successful music educator possesses four skills:

1. The ability to plan, both on paper and interactively, in the classroom setting.
2. The ability to format and pace lessons in a way that maximizes learning and minimizes frustration.
3. The ability to communicate with students in a variety of ways that enhance learning.
4. The ability to maintain a positive classroom atmosphere in which expectations are high and students are reinforced in their progress.

Certain similarities create a common theme in all of these data. Regardless of a researcher's findings, the qualities of enthusiasm, caring, communication, positive reinforcement, fair discipline, musical competency, and high professional standards serve as the suggested personality pillars of the successful band director.

Chapter 23

From Research to Reality

Even if you're on the right track, you won't get anywhere if you're standing still.

Will Rogers

Personal development is a way of life for students of human potential. Much like practicing an instrument to attain mastery, outstanding educators are always fine-tuning their communication skills and seeking more efficient and effective ways of bringing the art of music to their students. The combination of the contemporary findings of leadership with traditional band directing has offered an exciting new frontier of possibilities.

There is an ever-growing amount of data confirming that the educator can program his or her personality to ensure a higher degree of success in daily rehearsals as well as performances. Just as a pilot is required to go through a pre-flight checklist prior to flying a plane, the band director should have a pre-rehearsal checklist prior to standing in front of his or her students.

1. Will my present attitude promote a positive learning atmosphere?
2. Are all my thoughts focused on creating a musical experience throughout the rehearsal?
3. Do I exemplify the standards of excellence I expect from my students?

4. Am I properly prepared to make the best use of time by highlighting the musical growth of every student?

5. Have I dismissed my own agenda of personal considerations so that rehearsals will be directed toward serving students in a disciplined format of measured learning?

It is assumed that there will be an affirmative answer to these important pre-rehearsal questions, just as the pilot assumes that the airplane is mechanically ready to endure the requirements of flight. However, the mere process of reminding ourselves of the importance of our state of mind and the impact it will have on what can be accomplished during the upcoming rehearsal will afford us the opportunity to avoid any damaging attitude we might inadvertently bring to the rehearsal setting. We demand total concentration from the musicians and must, therefore, model this vital discipline. Pilots are not allowed to take off without a perfect score on the pre-flight checklist; directors should have a similar mandate before lifting their students to new heights.

Chapter 24

The Focal Point: Musical Prosperity for Band

The ones who miss all the fun
Are those who say, "It can't be done."
In solemn pride they stand aloof
And greet each venture with reproof.
Had they the power they'd efface
The history of the human race.
We'd have no radio or motor cars,
No street lit by electric stars;
No telegraph nor telephone,
We'd linger in the age of stone.
The world would sleep if things were run
By those who say, "It can't be done."

High-level achievement is attained when the synergy of the students and director is centered on a common goal. This can be accomplished through the guidance of the director based on four cornerstones of leadership effectiveness.

1. Make the students the emphasis of your teaching.

The more you can avoid relating your suggestions, corrections, thoughts, and comments in "I/me" terms, the more students will assume personal responsibility. Emphasize "we/us" and "you" in your verbal exchange. For example, "I think the trumpet phrase needs to have a gradual crescendo to establish more intensity prior to letter A. Do that for me," becomes, "Trumpets, you can generate some real excitement for us if you crescendo your line as you come up to letter A. We're counting on you."

Notice how the second instruction puts the responsibility on the players and offers them the chance to expressively contribute to the group, rather than simply "to do as they are told" to appease your request. They take ownership of the musical phrase and simultaneously become aware of their importance to their fellow musicians. The students are key in the process, for they bring life to the music. The director merely guides their energies toward achieving this mutually agreed-upon goal.

2. Explain clearly what you want from the performers.

Time is the director's most precious commodity and must be used judiciously. Any waste of time is a loss to everyone in the band. Communication skills—knowing what to say and how to say it—serve as the tools of every competent conductor. Avoid general comments that do not carry corrective instructions for improvement, i.e., "There is a balance problem in the brass. That's unacceptable; let's do it again," becomes, "Trombones, enter softly at letter G. You must be able to hear the clarinets." They now know exactly what to do, how to do it, and how to measure their success. (They must hear the clarinets.)

All too often students want to fulfill your instructional expectations but are really not aware of what to do. In place of asking, they will simply repeat their efforts until they either stumble accidentally on the right combination or just run out of time. Another cornerstone of leadership requires competent score preparation, which guarantees a more effective use of time.

3. Communicate throughout the rehearsal.

Communication is far more than words exchanged between playing segments. Communication can be verbal, visual, or tactile, and with music, band directors must incorporate intuitive connections with the musicians. Frequent eye contact is imperative, not with just first chair players, but with every section and member of the band. If musicians are expected to "watch the conductor," the conductor should share the responsibility by visually communicating with the musicians. A picture is worth a thousand words, and facial gestures will bring new dynamics to every rehearsal.

When the students are aware of this ongoing forum of communication, they will begin to communicate actively with the conductor. Only then can we "make music" as opposed to "playing notes." If the director is focused only on the score, the students will, likewise, focus only on their parts. The rehearsal then becomes a mechanical exercise and the human factor—the truly expressive component—disappears. The greater the frequency of genuine director-student communication during the rehearsal, the greater the musical experience.

4. Take responsibility for every condition in the rehearsal.

If there is a breakdown, an interruption, a discipline problem, or any other situation that threatens the rehearsal atmosphere, assume responsibility for it and move ahead. Stopping the band to justify, excuse, blame, or point out where someone's "wrong," preventing the intended rehearsal plan from taking place, is almost always an infringement on valuable group time. If an emergency class meeting or an unscheduled athletic event removes students from the rehearsal, embrace the situation, and do not amplify the problem by wasting class time with the remaining musicians.

Look for the possibilities the unexpected circumstances can provide, i.e., attention to certain sections of the music, listening to recordings, reviewing tapes, working on technique studies—and a myriad of other positive musical prospects. A verbal protest from the podium, dwelling on the obvious encroachment on the group's rehearsal time, only adds negative fuel to the present situation. Taking responsibility involves creatively using existing conditions to advance the cause of music for those students who are there, instruments in hand and ready to move ahead.

Chapter 25

Intrinsic and Extrinsic Rewards

*Your short-term actions multiplied by time
equals your long-term accomplishments.*

The joy of playing a musical instrument is an intrinsic experience. In every program, there are extrinsic rewards, but it is vital these bonuses be secondary in emphasis. If a student puts greater value on awards, chair placement, ratings, rankings, trips, or trophies than on musical experiences, the *product* takes precedence over the process. However, if the pleasure of playing the instrument is the priority, extrinsic prizes are merely personal premiums along the pathway of artistic expression.

Because of our often overly materialistic contemporary values, it is vitally important that the band director repeatedly explain why music is an integral part of our lives and stress the importance of the language of music. The director must constantly point out the benefits of mastering technical skills in order to provide an extended musical vocabulary of self-expression. Music accesses a part of the mind unique to every individual. It is a language unto itself; music can only be explained by music. It is, quite literally, feeling described in sound. The more technique available to the musician—i.e., the higher the musical vocabulary—the more successful he or she will be in communicating his or her innermost feelings. Therein lies the benefit of dedicated practice.

Do not assume that students will discover the *intrinsic dividends* on their own. Many promising young musicians give up studying music because they feel improperly compensated (with extrinsic payoffs) for their efforts and energies. For them, the success of their band experience is based solely on winning the contest, being selected as the soloist, appointed section leader, etc. They may be outstanding students committed to the band's success, but they consider playing their instrument as a means to the end, and when the end does not provide a satisfying extrinsic reward, they choose not to continue their study. In this case, everyone loses, particularly the student who quits. In contrast, if intrinsic value is a mainstay of the band experience, the extrinsic disappointments are far less damaging. Of course, there will be setbacks, but they should not be devastating to the individual's relationship with band or music. In this case, everyone wins, particularly the student who is ready to move on to the next level.

Chapter 26

Creating a Positive Climate for Learning

*Common sense in an uncommon degree is
what the world calls wisdom.*

Samuel Taylor Coleridge

Being in the band means devoting time to a common goal. It requires participants to relinquish much of their free time and/or fun time and reassign it to rehearsals. While many of their friends may enjoy the social benefits of adolescence, band students are fulfilling the requests of the band director. For a chosen few, the intrinsic payoff will warrant the dedication of their efforts and energies. Others, however, will seek additional dividends. All students are not *intrinsically motivated.* If they are properly trained, though, they will begin to comprehend a higher level of understanding, wean themselves from extrinsic payoffs, and enjoy music for the sake of music. Herein lies one of the most significant contributions a director can bring to any student: leading a child step by step to the joy of music. This metamorphosis will be almost immediate for some, but will require extended patience with others. Persistence alone is omnipotent in this charge. What classroom conditions best serve this goal?

Condition 1: Safety – Is the rehearsal a safe place to reside? Abraham Maslow's *Hierarchy of Needs* is very clear concerning the importance of survival; he states that survival is the basic human need, quickly followed by the need for safety. If the atmosphere of the rehearsal is threatening, students will put a higher priority on survival (avoidance of pain) and safety (maintaining their dignity) than on extending their talents and skills for the common goal of the ensemble. If the students and/or director assume a defensive posture, it is certain to hinder the group's musical objectives.

Condition 2: Challenge – Learning is exciting. Master teachers are well aware of the enthusiasm generated in an exchange of knowledge where student and teacher are both challenged. There is a fine art to establishing challenging, attainable goals without overwhelming the students with a barrage of information. Knowing each student learns at his or her own pace, the astute music teacher constantly regulates expectations to establish a challenge for gifted students while supporting the growth of those who might learn at a slower pace. Although it is difficult to explain how to establish this important teacher-student communication, it appears to fall in the ream of *intuitive sensitivity*. Experience itself could well be the key to mastering this skill. Beware the temptation to focus only on "fun and easy" material; it is deceptive both to the director and to the students. Quality begets quality. The mind left unchallenged will search for another source of inspiration.

Condition 3: Encouragement – To encourage means to bring into the presence of courage. Although there are times when every band director must confront an uncomfortable situation, admonishment or discouragement should not be the theme of the rehearsal. In most cases, students have chosen to participate in band above and beyond other academic requirements. Band often demands more of their time than other classes; therefore, it is important that the band director become a source of honest encouragement. Highlighting positive behavior is certain to develop a genuine sense of caring and sharing, an atmosphere conducive to musical expression. Encouragement is a necessity. It is the fuel students seek in their journey through life and can often be the deciding factor in lifting the student from the depths of rejection to the infinite possibilities of musical mastery. Do not underestimate the importance of encouragement; use it often to unleash the power to move the group forward.

Chapter 27

Professional Harmony: Our Key to Success

*Start by doing what's necessary, then what's possible,
and suddenly you are doing the impossible.*

St. Francis of Assisi

Some years ago, I was sitting in the Grand Ballroom at the Chicago Hilton & Towers awaiting one of the Midwest evening concerts and anticipating the classic words of wisdom shared by the designated master of ceremonies, John P. Paynter. As we all know, Mr. Paynter never missed a "teaching opportunity," and what greater classroom could there possibly be than the Midwest audience of directors and band enthusiasts? As he walked to the microphone, the crowd immediately came to a hush, demonstrating a true respect and honor for one of our profession's most revered heroes.

Mr. Paynter greeted everyone with one of his clever, humorous quips, then began his powerful lesson of the day. He gently, but firmly, reminded everyone of the need to "stand together" and avoid any temptation to engage in conversations that did not serve the positive growth and development of our students, our programs, or each other. He urged us to sidestep the cynical gossip that is often associated with the opinionated world of music. Then, in his trademark style, he said,

"Of course, none of *you* is guilty of this kind of behavior." He paused. The room filled with a deafening silence; it was evident *the master* was speaking to all of us, although I was certain he was aiming his reprimand directly at me. Mr. Paynter continued by borrowing this key phrase from Ben Franklin, "Folks, we either hang together, or we hang separately." He peered around the room, cocked his head, and (with his signature smile) added, "It's worth thinking about, isn't it?"

Less is more as proven by John Paynter's carefully chosen words.

Our rehearsal vocabulary focuses on harmony, balance, blend, unison, ensemble, etc. Countless hours are spent urging young players to "become one," to unselfishly commit their individual efforts and energies to a common goal, resulting in a higher attainment of musical expression. Through this process, we realize that *the total is greater than the sum of its parts*. It is, quite literally, what makes *a band, a chorus, or an orchestra*.

It's our likenesses that bring us together, but it's our differences that keep us together. Do we invite different opinions? Are we excited about new and contrasting philosophies? Do we open our minds to alternative viewpoints? Is there an unlimited space in our library of knowing for opposing thoughts and beliefs? Can we agree to disagree and still support one another? Is harmony merely a musical term, or is it a fundamental value we exercise in our professional lives?

It is always comfortable and fun to work with those with whom we agree, but we learn when we are confronted with an opposing viewpoint. Rather than put up the wall of denial, wouldn't we be best served with the logic and thought process employed by our counterparts? We might discover new data that would change or modify our own thinking, or we may become more certain of our original judgment; either outcome is certain to strengthen both parties.

In many ways, the professional athletic community demonstrates *harmony* in a remarkable fashion, particularly considering that they live (and thrive) in a competitive arena. People throughout the world spend countless hours cheering their favorite team to victory, arguing the strength of this or that player, demonstrating their fanship with everything from souvenir jerseys to logo bumper stickers. All the while, those in charge gather regularly to ensure there is a balance of talent throughout the league. They know the success of their endeavor is solely dependent on the support of one another. The overriding priority of the group is the health and welfare of all those who have decided to be a part of their forum. They have chosen to *hang together.* There will be no fans without a game; there will be no game without a consensus among the players, coaches, and owners; they *must hang together.* It is this fundamental understanding that has propelled the sports culture to such a prominent place in our society. Their degree of *cooperation* far exceeds their portrayed agenda of *competition.*

This is not to suggest we all meet in a big room and create a free-agent agreement to ensure balanced instrumentation for our bands, although the idea does have some merit, doesn't it? However, we can see the value of *cooperative harmony* as it relates to our professional goals; in addition, by comparison we can clearly observe the negative damage that results from internal discord. This was and is the foundation of Mr. Paynter's plea; his perspective allowed him to see how vital we are to one another.

While we may have strong disagreements and opposing opinions, aren't we all eager to see our students experience the joys of musical excellence? Isn't that the *likeness* that brings us together? And the way we go about achieving this common goal represents the *differences* that keep us together. Ultimately, the *key* is to support one another, for within this context is the potential for unlimited growth for our profession, our programs, and—most importantly—our students.

Just as Mr. Paynter said, "We either hang together, or we hang separately." *It's worth thinking about, isn't it?*

Chapter 28

Cooperation Creates Victory

Together we stand, divided we fall.

We are a society that thrives on *competition*. We *compete* in school for grades; we *compete* in our professional lives to achieve positions and titles; and we compete in our daily life patterns for everything from a faster lane on the freeway to a winning number in the local lottery. We like to win, to get ahead, to maneuver ourselves to a better vantage point. Perhaps Darwin's proposed theory in his popular writing *Survival of the Fittest* clearly evidences our competitive spirit, our ongoing, ever-present striving to get to the front of the pack. It is powerful motivational fuel for humans, but like any energy force, *competition* can be used in a positive or negative fashion.

Observing the positive enthusiasm generated by *competition in athletics,* other disciplines have quickly jumped on the bandwagon. Our schools now have science fairs, 4-H shows, debate clubs, essay contests, and music festivals recognizing the achievements of an array of talents ranging from a flute solo to a 400-piece marching band.

The good news is all of these organized *competitive forums* have created much excitement; however, we must be clearly aware that there can be a down side to the *win-at-all-costs* attitude. As educators, the cautionary responsibility rests directly on our shoulders. Take heed, for the instant gratification of first place can become a haunting detriment when it alone is the only measure of accomplishment.

When we ask students to "go the extra mile" by committing their valuable time to the art of music making, we must focus on the *intrinsic benefits* they will gain as a result of their investment, rather than the *extrinsic rewards* that come as a by-product of their dedication. If "getting first place" is more important than the joy of an inspired performance (whatever the adjudication outcome) then it is time to do some philosophical reprioritizing. Is the goal to add more trophies of achievement to the shelves in the rehearsal room or to stretch the students to a new level of artistic communication? The musical growth of the students must stand as the top priority in every instance.

Over the years, the ongoing debate about the value of competition (in our musical world) has caused many music educators to avoid any aspect of adjudication/evaluation. Much like the ostrich with its head in the sand, this may be a overreaction or escape; it may also be an unrealistic approach to preparing our students to address the realities of life. At the same time, if everything from chair-placement to a solo audition is couched in a competitive framework, the need to beat the fellow musician takes precedence over the personal growth and development gained by a solid practice-program of healthy self-discipline. The key to a successful balance is achieved through the careful guidance of the teacher. Instead of dangling the proverbial competitive carrot in front of the students, we might be better served if we rewarded and recognized their successful habits and patterns.

For example:

1. **Resolving a problem.** Many students are quick to recognize or identify problems, but there are few who will come up with a resolution. Those who do should be put in the spotlight and given responsibilities within the program.

2. **Making decisions and taking action.** There are many who "wait to be told what to do," then do it remarkably well. Look for those who go one step beyond and are willing to take a stand, make a choice, and follow-through on their decisions; herein lie the leaders of tomorrow.

3. **Loyalty.** In today's world, loyalty is a treasured attribute. Competition is the test of one's loyalty, not when we win, but when we lose. To avoid the, "If we can't win, I quit!" attitude, reinforce the character strength of loyalty.

4. **Cooperation.** Nothing is impossible when a group of individuals chooses to make *cooperation* the theme of the working atmosphere. Alternately, it is almost impossible to move any group forward when they are constantly competing to gain the upper hand on their fellow performers.

It is apparent that we needn't beat another person or persons to *win;* we simply need to improve ourselves to experience the intrinsic victory that is a result of learning, growing, and *becoming.* To this end, let us continue to support one another in the ongoing exploration of artistic expression and realize the value of competition is merely a stepping stone for our students to witness others who share a similar passion. When all is said and done, we must band together if we ever hope to attain true victory.

Chapter 29

A Template for Success

Amateurs practice until they get it right; professionals practice until they can't get it wrong.

As we examine today's most successful directors/leaders, there are some obvious key characteristics that serve as cornerstones that we can highlight and adapt to our own situations:

1. **Present an inspiring and compelling mission.** Instead of merely "working to get better," outstanding directors constantly communicate the group's shared goals. While elevating the musical standards, they create an ongoing awareness of various ways to support the ensemble's vision. The long-range goals are always at the forefront of their communication, allowing the students to focus on the self-imposed behaviors required to achieve the organizational mission.

2. **Demonstrate proven disciplines necessary to create group synergy.** The emphasis is on the "power of the people" rather than the strict authoritarian rule of the director. The energy of the students serves as the fuel for forward motion. Discipline is an outgrowth of the commitment of the group members; instead of "being told what to do," the students are challenged to develop their own parameters of behavior that will support the program from bottom to top.

Positive discipline renewal comes from an ongoing series of group questions such as:

- What is working well for us and why is it working?
- How could we better serve the people, the group, the goals?
- What behavior will best support those around us?
- What behaviors are counterproductive? How can we alter them?

Blame is discouraged; solutions and options are encouraged.

3. Put people first. The young musicians, students, and members of the group are the source of unlimited growth and development. It becomes the director's responsibility to unleash the knowledge, creativity, and talent inherent in every member. This requires an ongoing interaction among everyone associated with the program; an open and honest line of communication confirms the director's concern for the welfare of the musicians.

4. Model a high degree of self-responsibility. The "Do as I say, not as I do" theme is not as effective in today's educational setting. It is important for the director to take responsibility for mistakes and share credit for successes. Modeling is still the most potent method of teaching and leading; therefore, it is imperative that the successful director demonstrate trust, appreciation, caring, and concern. The master teacher and/or educator understands that it is not necessary to have the answers to all questions, but that strength often comes from saying, "I don't know. Let's find the answer together."

5. Have high expectations for results. The modern-day successful band directors are both people-oriented and results-oriented. They focus on the dual task of "taking care of people" and "creating results through those people." While accepting who people are, they do not accept behavior that does not support the goal of quality. This delicate balance is an ongoing learning process for the director and the ensemble; it is constantly changing, shifting, becoming.

6. Create a culture of quality through leadership/modeling. One of the most difficult challenges directors face has little to do with the actual teaching of music; it concerns the establishment of a positive learning atmosphere that encourages the members of the group to contribute without fear of embarrassment, reprimand, pain, etc. If the students assume a defensive posture to protect themselves, it becomes impossible to access their creative potential; however, if the director consistently models a forward-focused discipline, a remarkable shift in attitudes, energy, and performance can be felt. There will be a dramatic improvement recognized in every facet of the rehearsal climate and performance achievement.

About the Author

Tim Lautzenheiser is a well-known name in the music education world as a teacher, clinician, author, composer, consultant, adjudicator, and, above all, a trusted friend to anyone interested in working with young people in developing a desire for excellence.

His own career involves ten years of successful college band directing at Northern Michigan University, the University of Missouri, and New Mexico State University. During this time, Tim developed highly acclaimed groups in all areas of the instrumental and vocal field.

Following three years in the music industry, he created Attitude Concepts for Today, an organization designed to manage the many requests for workshops, seminars, and convention speaking engagements on positive attitude and effective leadership training. He presently holds the Earl Dunn Distinguished Lecturer position at Ball State University. Tim is also the director of education for Conn-Selmer, and he serves as the national spokesperson for MENC's "Make A Difference with Music" program.

Tim's other books published by GIA Publications, *The Art of Successful Teaching: A Blend of Content & Context* and *The Joy of Inspired Teaching*, are bestsellers in the music profession. He is also coauthor of Hal Leonard's popular band method, Essential Elements, as well as the creator of the highly-acclaimed *Director's Communication Kits*.

Tim is a graduate of Ball State University and the University of Alabama. He was awarded an honorary doctorate from VanderCook College of Music. Additional awards include the distinguished Sudler Order of Merit from the John Philip Sousa Foundation, Mr. Holland's Opus Award, and the Music Industry Award from the Midwest Clinic Board of Directors.